THE SELLING FORMULA

**5 STEPS FOR
INSTANT SALES IMPROVEMENT**

THE
SELLING
FORMULA

BRIAN W. ROBINSON

LIONCREST
PUBLISHING

THE SELLING FORMULA
5 Steps for Instant Sales Improvement

ISBN   978-1-61961-880-0 *Paperback*
         978-1-61961-881-7 *Ebook*
         978-1-61961-882-4 *Audiobook*

This book is dedicated to:

My amazing wife, Cindy, whose example of consistent love and perseverance—even in the midst of monumental challenges— has motivated, humbled, and changed me forever.

And to my precious children: James, Corey, Aubrey, Lindsay, Christian, Joseph, Grace, and Gabrielle. You are each the greatest blessing a father could ever hope for, and the greatest inspiration for working as hard as it takes to provide a great future.

I love you all more than words can possibly describe.

CONTENTS

INTRODUCTION

The Selling Formula has been crafted and refined over a 20-year period that included countless days and miles on the road. Missing family events. No-show appointments that had been confirmed. Sleepless nights. Cold-calling in sunshine, rain, snow, sleet, and freezing cold.

Years of sales training, sales mentoring, sales development, and thousands of hours reading books and listening to tapes, CDs, and podcasts on the subject of selling.

It cost years in hotel rooms, meeting rooms, board rooms, and offices. Endless sales meetings and conference calls. Follow-up emails. Follow-up phone calls. Wanting to quit. Getting up and doing it again. Wanting to quit. Getting up and doing it again. Thousands of sales presentations. Thankless no's and, Thank God, yes's, too.

A serious price was paid to get this into your hands. I hope you handle this information with care, because it could change your life.

CHAPTER 1

TODAY

He knew he was about to die.

Driving 75 miles an hour over a bridge, he hit a patch of black ice that caused his car to do a 180-degree spin. Now he was going backwards at 75 miles an hour.

Utterly helpless and hurtling toward the edge of a 30-foot embankment, in his side-view mirror, he saw the shoulder of the road pass underneath his car. At almost the same instant, his mirror was torn off by a metal reflector that marked the edge of the road. Then, incredibly, he came to a complete stop.

Looking out the driver's-side window, he realized the wet snow pack had caused his car to sink just enough to stop him from plunging down the steep embankment.

After taking a moment to regain his composure, he called a towing company. About 25 minutes later, he was pulled out of the snow and continued his trip to Kansas City, with the mirror dangling from the side of the car.

I was the driver of that car. There could have been a dramatically different outcome, but my life was spared.

There's no guarantee you'll see tomorrow. You're here for a reason. You're reading this book for a reason.

Today is all you have.

Therefore, I challenge you to take one idea from this book and implement it today.

Not next week, or next month, or when the seasons change, or when the economy is better, or when there's a full moon, or when management changes, or when you get "lucky." Luck is a myth anyway.

You may be in the top 1% of your industry, the bottom 10%, or somewhere in between: it doesn't matter. You can get more deals done by applying just one new concept from this book on your next sales call—today.

You don't have to stay where you are, even if you're at the top of your game.

Why wait 30, 60, or 90 days when you can choose right now to change one thing you're doing? That one thing, applied faithfully and consistently, could literally double, triple, or quadruple your outcomes and income. How would that feel?

You can choose to get more deals done right now.

WHAT YOU'LL GET FROM THIS BOOK

If you're looking for the latest consultative, collaborative, and customer-centric approach to selling in the twenty-first century, you won't find it here. Truth is: the best salespeople have always been consultative, collaborative, and customer-centric.

The tenets of selling are timeless: they're finding your prospect's needs and providing a solution to meet them.

What you will get is a battle-tested and proven five-step selling process that will give you greater confidence, clarity, and closing power, so you can get more deals done, make more money, and have a greater impact in your own life and the lives of others.

Plus, The Selling Formula works in both face-to-face and phone-sales situations. I know, because I've sold millions of dollars of products and services and have never personally met 90% of my clients, other than speaking with them by phone.

Also, in the second bonus chapter at the end of the book, you will get The Assumptive Appointment Solution™ with the exact scripts I used to set appointments and grow my business from $0 to $40,000 per month in the first 12 months of selling.

And if you go to TheSellingFormula.com, you can download the free step-by-step Direct Mail Lead Generation Guide, which details exactly how you can transition from cold-calling prospects to their asking you to call them, while virtually eliminating all those painful hours of travel.

THE DIFFERENCE-MAKER

What's the difference between great salespeople and all the others?

It's you.

You and your personality, your character, your questions, your willingness to learn, your passion, your drive to continually refine and enhance your sales process, your willingness to serve, your willingness to make your prospect uncomfortable when necessary, and your willingness to ask for business.

When I first started selling in a straight-commission environment, I'd call my associate to recap the day, and if one of us said, "I had a lot of great presentations today," the other one would say, with a laugh, "Yeah, I didn't sell anything either."

Bottom line: we are paid to close deals.

We all want to find a way to be more effective to better provide for ourselves and our families, while receiving recognition and making a difference in the world.

Below the surface, however, the question that tends to haunt us is: are we courageous, disciplined, and brave enough to do it? Deep down, we wonder if we have what it takes to be great.

Are we "worthy" of the success we desire, or will we sabotage that success by pulling back when we get out of our comfort zone?

Will our dedication, discipline, and hard work win the day?

Will our prospects buy from us?

Maybe they will, and maybe they won't. But I can tell you this with absolute certainty: you can dramatically increase the odds of them buying from you by adopting a rock-solid sales process that's consistent and repeatable every time you speak with a prospect.

Before we get into that, I'd like to give you the back story on the biggest transition I ever made in my life: going from corporate America to an entrepreneurial startup where, if I didn't sell, I didn't eat.

THE DREAM

One night, I had a vivid dream that I was being drafted into the military.

As it began, I was walking into a plain, beige, cinder-block building with a line of other men. All of us were wearing only one thing, boxer shorts, so there was a definite sense of vulnerability.

We were waiting in line to get our boots and military fatigues.

As I walked into the building, there was a woman sitting

on a stool. The stool was high above me. So high, in fact, I felt like she was towering over me as I looked up at her. A single bare light bulb hung from the middle of the concrete ceiling overhead.

As she leaned down and handed me my military fatigues and boots—and I remember this very clearly—she said, "Mr. Robinson, I want you to know that you will no longer eat when you want to eat, drink when you want to drink, or do what you want to do. We will tell you everything that you'll do."

Then the dream abruptly ended.

I was so disturbed by and desperate to know what the dream meant that I spent the next morning replaying it over and over in my mind and praying for understanding.

Back when the draft was active in the United States, military service required a two-year commitment, whether you wanted to join or not. If your draft number was chosen, you were going to serve in the armed forces.

After a while, the meaning became clear: the dream was a "heads-up" about the commitment level that was going to be required to leave corporate America and help start a new company.

I was getting ready to enter a period of my life that would require at least a two-year commitment, without any possibility of turning back.

I would be learning to submit myself to an entirely different lifestyle and level of trust in God's provision than I'd ever experienced before.

Little did I know at the time, I would also experience a humbling of severe proportions.

I also knew deep down this was ultimately going to be an experience that, while difficult, would bring great personal and professional growth. As much pain as I might encounter as a result, I was going to be better for it in the end.

But that didn't make things any easier.

When recruiters called with opportunities to interview for stable jobs with major corporations back in the medical field—and I received many—I declined for no other reason than that dream. But I'd be lying if I told you that I didn't want to go back.

Why didn't I go back, then?

Because I just couldn't. I wouldn't. I was doing what I had to do.

What I quickly learned is that, to succeed, I would have to develop a process that reliably worked almost every time I was in a sales conversation. That process is what you're going to be introduced to in this book.

WHO AM I?

I'm the youngest of three kids who grew up in a predominantly Catholic neighborhood about 15 miles from downtown Chicago.

I went to college right out of high school, grabbed the so-called golden ring with a major corporation—Coca-Cola USA—worked with them for three-and-a-half years cutting my teeth in sales, and then went to work with Johnson & Johnson. During this time, when my wife and I were right in the middle of raising our children, I went to night school to get my MBA.

Speaking of which, I am the father of eight children—I guess growing up in a Catholic neighborhood rubbed off on me—and the husband of one amazing wife.

All my work has been in sales, marketing, training, and consulting.

With Johnson & Johnson, I worked in four separate divisions, starting out in the Patient Care division, where we sold wound-care products on hospital nursing floors. Among those items were bandages and other wound recovery-related products. From there, I moved into the Surgical Specialties division, where we sold products that helped surgeons stop bleeding in the brain, thoracic, and abdominal cavities.

My next assignment, the crown jewel of the divisions, was Ethicon Endo-Surgery. We taught surgeons how to improve laparoscopy procedures—surgery conducted through ports using a video camera. The surgeons knew how to do this, of course, but we helped them do their job better with our products, services, and training, which ultimately provided better outcomes in the operating room. I spent seven years in that division as a top performer, before moving on to help start a new division called "Biopsis," which was designed around minimally invasive breast biopsies.

Instead of taking a lump of tissue out of a woman's breast to determine if it was cancerous, we used a device called the "Mammotome," which, with ultrasound or x-ray guidance, targeted the area of concern and extracted a tiny specimen that the physician examined for cancer. It was much less invasive than other diagnostic options. I established a hands-on connection with the radiologists I worked with, as well as with patients who would often be staring up at me, eyes wide open, while the procedure was being done.

In some ways, I'd reached the pinnacle of medical sales in terms of physician and patient interaction.

I had penetrated about 85% of my territory. Getting the other 15% would have provided significantly diminishing returns compared to the time invested, and I had reached a certain comfort level. So, I worked just a few days each week, and worked hard, of course, but soon got bored.

I was tired of building equity in a large corporation. I wanted the opportunity to build equity in my own business, which felt like the next logical step. I had spent a combined 15 years working in the corporate sales and marketing world, with Coca-Cola USA and Johnson & Johnson, and was ready to move on into something entrepreneurial.

THE STARTUP OPPORTUNITY

Then one day, a friend of mine who was starting a new

company selling on-hold messages—the messages you get when you call a business and get put on hold, which promote other products and services—approached me and asked if I'd join him.

After four months of consideration and considerable prayer with my wife, it was time to make the jump.

I gave up the company car, benefits, recognition as a top performer, and instant credibility that comes along with working for a world-renowned multi-billion-dollar company and went to work with a friend who had less than $150,000 in annual sales for a service that, honestly, businesses rarely think they want or need.

STARTING ALL OVER

I had come from 15 years of a guaranteed salary plus commissions, and now had to hunt and kill what I was going to eat, with no salary as a safety net. Well actually, I did have a salary, but it was totally dependent upon my friend and me selling enough to pay for it, while still servicing our clients.

I was excited and scared to death, but learned to embrace the struggle and do what it took to set appointments, show the service, and close deals. It was a steep learning curve.

The new reality was that I had to keep moving no matter what. I had to get leads. I had to set appointments. I had to close deals. I had to make things happen, or I was going to get crushed by a freight train bearing down on me: the freight train of no deals and no cash flow.

This do-or-die reality forced me to create The Selling Formula process.

My stress levels, of course, now reflected this new world of straight commission-selling. Not that it wasn't stressful at Johnson & Johnson or Coca-Cola; both were highly competitive and intense environments.

With Johnson & Johnson, for example, I would be in the operating room during a laparoscopic procedure, and the surgeon might ask me to verify the anatomical landmarks within the abdomen to confirm, via video camera, where he should make the next move with his surgical instruments.

Now, there's some pressure there for sure, and it was important to be what we called "mentally scrubbed." But that was a different kind of stress—a hold-your-breath moment of nerves, rather than a constant drumbeat of knowing that if I don't sell, I don't eat.

On straight commission, I experienced firsthand the

difference between the proverbial commitment level of the chicken and the pig regarding breakfast: the chicken is "interested;" the pig is "committed." As a straight-commission salesperson, you're committed.

THE REALITY

Here was the situation: I was given a copy of Microsoft Streets and Trips to put on my laptop, a book of all the bank contacts in Kansas and Nebraska, and told to go sell.

It was just me and my friend out on the road, going in different directions, then calling each other at night from our hotels to debrief.

We set appointments via a process we called "cold-call assumptive appointment-setting." We put the bank locations into Streets and Trips, picked a bank contact in a city, called, and told them we'd be in town on a specific day and time and would like 10 minutes to show them what we were doing with other banks just like theirs.

If they agreed to the appointment, we looked in Streets and Trips to see the next-closest bank, called them, and referenced the appointment we just made, in hopes of generating curiosity—"If he's going to meet with them, maybe I should too."—and set another appointment.

I'm greatly simplifying this for the sake of brevity, but we had a very specific script we'd follow. Often, we would just leave a voicemail telling the prospect we'd be in town; then, as a courtesy, ask them to call us if they couldn't make the appointment. We assumed the appointment was set if we didn't hear from them, and would then drive hundreds of miles, often confirming as we drove. Pretty crazy, but about 70% of our appointments would hold.

If the appointment didn't show, we went to the next one on our agenda for the day or tried to fill it with other cold calls.

SOMETHING HAD TO CHANGE

The first year was an endless cycle of cold-call assumptive appointment-setting, while being away from home three to four days a week and logging 1,000 to 1,500 miles of drive time. As they say, I was living the dream: stressed out, exhausted, and disconnected from my family.

By the way, to add even more excitement to the transition, when I started the job my wife was three months pregnant. I remember calling her from a conference to see how her ultrasound went at the doctor's office that day. She said, "Well, the baby looks good!" I chatted with her a little longer, and as I was about to hang up the phone she added, "And the other one does too!"

The other one?

"Yes!" she said, "We're going to have twins!" Wow. We were going to have babies number seven and eight! I was overwhelmed with...a need to drink a beer...or two.

Now, with eight kids, you're probably asking yourself if I know what causes this pregnancy thing. And I do, thank you very much.

When our twin girls were born, I had been with the new company six months. We literally don't remember the first year of their lives with them, as we survived on about four hours of sleep per night.

So, here we were: my wife was at home with our eight kids, ages 14 and under, trying to take care of newborn twin babies, while I was traveling three to four days a week. She was seriously drowning, and I was barely keeping my head above water. It was overwhelming. Something had to change.

So, my search for an answer began.

I had to do two things: consistently generate leads and sell them without leaving my office.

FREE RECORDED MESSAGES?

I had just purchased an audio series by Joe Polish and Tim Paulson entitled "Piranha Marketing" and was listening to it as I was driving to Kansas.

Joe and Tim were sharing their idea of free recorded messages for lead generation. You write a script, record the message on a toll-free number, then drive your prospects to that message to generate warm leads. No more cold-calling.

When I heard the idea, I literally stopped what I was listening to and yelled out loud, "That's the answer!" I called my friend and told him that this was going to revolutionize how I generated leads and help get me off the road. So, I got to work recording a message on one of the extensions at our office to test the concept.

To drive prospects to the message, I asked one of my bank associations if they would do a fax blast to their members—yes, a fax blast. Guess what happened? The calls started coming in immediately. Our receptionist was overwhelmed with calls. People listened to the message and left voicemails asking to find out more. It was amazing!

Over the years, my lead-generation process has evolved into hand-addressed direct mail driving recipients to a landing page with a video that, on average, provides a five-to-one return on investment. You can obtain a copy of this process by going to TheSellingFormula.com.

For the first time, I had real hope that I could get off the road and sell from my office. But now the challenge was that I'd never sold anything over the phone before.

The fact that I would have to present our service by phone required that I develop a very deliberate process. Everything from initial rapport-building to interviewing the prospect, reviewing our solution, and closing the deal had to be fine-tuned.

Not only that, I was now only able to use one feedback source: my prospect's voice. No more facial expressions, eye movement, body language, or office environment.

Did it work? Yes, it did. And I'm going to give you the formula in Chapter 3. But first, let's take a quick look at the truth about selling.

CHAPTER 2

DESTINED FOR GREATER THINGS

Selling: one of the most emotionally exhilarating, challenging, and potentially terrifying vocations you can choose—aside from parenting. With eight kids of my own, I know what I'm talking about.

Some of the many challenges of selling include:

- Consistently "showing up" every day, regardless of how you feel
- Staying sharp mentally and physically
- Being fully aware of your inner dialogue, so as not to embrace negative thoughts
- Constant lead-generation that may require daily cold-calling

- Travel that can easily consume the better part of your week for just a few hours of key meetings
- Exceeding quota every month
- Thoroughly knowing your competition and staying ahead of their moves
- Showing professionalism, regardless of whether you're exhausted, overwhelmed, have been told no for the tenth time in a row, or are dealing with challenges at home or sickness in your own body

WHY DO PEOPLE GET INTO SALES?

So, why do people get into the sales profession? Sometimes, it's a last resort option. For those who choose this profession, ultimately, it's about freedom. That's the promise of sales. Sell more. Make more. Theoretically, there's no cap on your income.

You're told that it's a numbers game, and if you make X number of cold calls, this will yield Y number of appointments which will yield Z number of sales.

Seemed reasonable when you heard it—didn't it? But have you ever felt like something's missing from that equation?

Well, there is. The quality of your lead-generation process and your own effectiveness in your sales process has everything to do with the sum of that equation: the number of deals closed. Oh, and it also helps if you're selling a good product or service—that's a given.

Because, if you don't believe in what you're selling right now—move on. Life is too short to waste your time trying to convince others to purchase something that you really don't believe in.

DESTINED FOR GREATER THINGS

Whether you're a top sales veteran or someone who's new to the profession, you may have this gnawing sense that you were destined for greater things.

Perhaps you're doing very well and just want some new tips and techniques for your professional sales tool bag.

Or, perhaps you're thinking that your selling breakthrough is just around the corner, and if you can keep your head down and just gut it out for the next three, six, or 12 months, the freedom you long for will be waiting with arms wide open.

Maybe you're just flat out exhausted, because you feel like you're pushing rocks uphill all day long. The joy and exhilaration of closing a deal may only last for a moment.

Then you remember you can't rest there and enjoy it very long, because there's a big freakin' freight train coming down the tracks.

It's right behind you, and if you don't keep running—and running hard—you're going to get crushed.

Sales over. Game over. The end.

If only you could get some margin in your life, then maybe, just maybe, you could actually think about new ways to present your product or service. Or maybe you could try prospecting differently or focus on a different vertical market.

But then you wonder, "What if I try something different and it doesn't work and the freight train just gets closer?"

So, then you recommit to digging deeper, trying harder, and doing more of what you've already been doing, while hoping and praying for a better result.

Truly, that *IS* insanity. I get it. I've been there.

In fact, what I just described is how I lived for years.

As a straight-commission salesperson, my life felt like

one series of stress-bound sales moments after another, punctuated by a few days of peace—or maybe a week when I was on vacation, which required the first three days just to start coming down off the ledge I was living on, and begin getting some rest. Then, after coming home, the cycle would start all over again.

I literally wound up getting heart surgery from it all. I'd like for you to avoid the same outcome.

Because, if you're living like this, the fact is, you really haven't left work when you leave work.

Your thoughts are consumed with replaying a presentation you had or your sales funnel or what deals will actually get signed. Or you're wondering why that prospect who seemed so interested and engaged is suddenly not calling you back or returning your emails.

Seriously, what's up with that?

And you know, just like water over a dam, all this stress and the resulting disconnection spills into your home life, your outside activities, your relationship with your spouse and your kids, who pull mom aside and ask her for the umpteenth time, "What's wrong with dad?" Or who ask dad, "What's wrong with mom?"

They're confused, because they don't know which version of you they're going to get when you walk in the door: the intense, sullen, stressed-out version, or the happy, smiling, carefree version.

I'm here to tell you there's a way out of this mess. That's why I wrote this book for you.

You were destined for greater things. And if you take the content in these pages seriously, you will most definitely achieve greater things.

WHAT DO YOU NEED?

Maybe you need better closing skills or a dose of confidence or better probing questions.

Maybe you need to better match and mirror your client's behavior to increase trust and rapport.

Maybe you need to bring a higher level of value to your prospect and become the best educator in your sales space.

Or perhaps you need a rock-solid means of generating leads without constant cold-calling.

You could be one step away from greatness, but can you identify which step it should be?

The point is that you're following a sales process right now.

The question is: does your sales process continually and consistently contribute to your success?

The only way to know is to identify the process you follow now. And ultimately, that is going to be either your process or your prospect's.

Here are a few questions to consider:

How did you learn your current sales approach? Was it formal training from your employer? Was it the sink-or-swim method, where you just got thrown out on the street and had to figure it out?

Was it gleaned from mentors or sales coaches, the school of hard knocks, books, and podcasts?

Do you know why you do what you do now?

Could you articulate the steps?

We will explore this in the chapters that follow. But first, let me introduce you to The Selling Formula.

CHAPTER 3

THE SELLING FORMULA

There's a saying in the sales and marketing world that you need to figure out what keeps your prospect awake at 2:00 a.m., then enter the conversation they're already having in their mind with an answer to their problem, and they will buy your solution. I can assure you, having on-hold messages was not what my prospects were lying awake worrying about at 2:00 a.m.

However, this formula, if faithfully implemented, works in an environment in which people do not even think they want what you're selling—where they don't think that a need for your product or service even exists.

I know this because virtually no one I initially spoke to

honestly thought they wanted or needed on-hold messages for their phone system—since they didn't believe
they put people on hold in the first place.

Nonetheless, the components of this formula have personally helped me consistently sell more than $1.5 million
a year almost entirely without leaving my office.

In fact, I was the first person in the history of the on-hold
message industry to sell over $1 million dollars in 12
months by phone—without any cold-calling.

IS WHAT YOU'RE DOING NOW WORKING FOR YOU?

So, I'm just curious—on a scale of one to 10, with 10 being
the best, how well is what you're doing right now working
for you?

Stop and answer that question.

What would it take to move your selling effectiveness to a
10? As I mentioned, whether you realize it or not, you're
following a sales process.

We are creatures of habit, and I know as well as you
do that at least 80%, and more likely 90%, of what
you're doing on a daily basis in your sales conver-

sations, and your life, is consistently the same—for better or worse.

My goal is to help you identify the most important steps you could take in your current sales process and improve upon and refine them to catapult your sales to the next level.

Maybe you're doing well right now, but you have this nagging suspicion that you could be doing even better. I want to help you isolate that suspicion and focus on it. Uncovering the root of that suspicion could reveal the difference that would make your sales go from good to great.

Take a good, hard look at your sales process from beginning to end and ask yourself which component you're most uncomfortable with. Where do you tighten up? What makes you feel stressed? Where are you most concerned? Because whichever point that is, that's exactly the area you will want to address first.

IT'S YOUR PROCESS OR THE PROSPECT'S

Unless you're sticking to your own well-articulated sales process, you are defaulting to the prospect's process, which sounds much like this:

"So, Mr. Salesman, tell me what you've got and how much it costs?" Silently, the prospect stares at you, arms folded.

"Well," you reply, "we provide a..."

"Yeah, well what is it? And how much does it cost?"

You share the price.

"Yeah, that's too much, I'm really not interested."

You're completely on your heels, while the prospect is directing the conversation.

However, if you have your own process, you won't be tempted to simply vomit up the price and then hope the prospect is interested.

Instead, you stick to your process and provide a much more helpful experience for that prospect and yourself.

I've often had a prospect ask the same two questions, "What have you got and how much does it cost?"

"That's a great question," I'll reply. "And I will share exactly what the pricing is, but here's what I've discovered: unless you have some context for exactly what I'm offering, the pricing won't make a lot of sense.

"Furthermore, I don't have enough information to know if you qualify for our service. So, with your permission, what I'd like to do is ask you some questions first, then I'd be happy to provide you with pricing information. Is that fair enough?"

Most level-headed people will say, "OK. Yeah, that's fair." Some people will persist and say, "I don't care, I want to know what it costs, because I don't know if we can do business together. I don't care how great this is..."

I'll address the answer to that scenario in the chapters that follow.

But first, let's take a look at the components of The Selling Formula. Then we'll move into an explanation for each of the steps.

THE SELLING FORMULA STEPS
STEP 1: CONNECT AND SET AGENDA
Connect

The first component of every great sales conversation, and really any conversation, is to connect with the person you're speaking to quickly and sincerely. It boils down to treating other people in a way that honors and shows you care about them.

You'll discover:

- How to put yourself into a great pre-call mindset
- Why you should "like" and "care" about your prospect before you ever meet them
- The power of matching and mirroring
- Simple yet powerful rapport-building questions
- What your role as a sales professional is

Set Agenda

Tell the prospect where you're going with your conversation. If done correctly, this one thing could easily explode your sales. It did for me.

You'll see:

- Why you need an agenda for your sales call
- How to share the agenda—sample script
- What three points to include in your agenda

STEP 2: INTERVIEW

This is the most important step in the process. You ask specific, preplanned questions, take notes on the answers given, and uncover the gap, problem, frustration, or need that your offer will solve.

In this step, you'll find out:

- Why the quality of your questions will make or break your sales conversation
- How to develop great questions
- How to put your questions in the right order
- What to say to easily transition to the interview step— this may seem trivial, but is a big deal
- What to say as you begin the interview that answers the prospect's question, "Why should I listen to you?"
- Why you should take notes with pen and paper—not a laptop—on every sales call
- What "sales malpractice" is and how to avoid it
- What to do if someone insists that you give them pricing up front without letting you ask questions first

STEP 3: PRESENT YOUR SOLUTION

You set up the conversation to focus on the key components of your offering, then educate your prospect with best practices, stories, and other evidence that show you have the answer to the problems you uncovered in the interview.

We'll dive into:

- Two key reasons why you need to provide an overview of where you're going in this step
- Exactly what to say to transition from the interview to educating the prospect on your solution
- What every prospect wants to know about you and why
- Why you want your prospect to take notes
- The most important way to educate your prospect
- How to set yourself apart from your competitors
- How to become invaluable to your prospect

STEP 4: PRICING AND GUARANTEES

In this step, we'll look at:

- The power of presenting your pricing and guarantees together
- The power of offering three price options
- Why your prospects want choices instead of just one price
- Why you should offer a guarantee
- What you can guarantee
- How to create a killer guarantee

STEP 5: CLOSE THE DEAL

With this final step in The Selling Formula, you'll discover:

- What closing is
- Why you should always attempt to have some deadline with a special offer
- How to present your special offer along with your pricing
- How to introduce a one-time incentive to get a deal closed
- Why "I have to think it over" is the same as getting a no, and what to do about it
- How to quit chasing your prospects for an answer once and for all
- How to get prospects who are ignoring you to respond almost immediately
- Why your prospect's fear of loss is your greatest opportunity to close a deal
- How you can double your closing ratio with one simple question

Now, let's look at the first step in The Selling Formula.

CHAPTER 4

CONNECT AND SET AGENDA

In this chapter, I'm going to review how connecting with your prospect always starts before you walk into a meeting or make the first phone call.

I'll also talk about the power of having a pre-call ritual that you go through to get into the proper mental and emotional state to best connect with your prospect.

Then I'll show you three easy ways to subconsciously create better rapport with your prospect, the result of which will be higher trust and likeability.

Next, I'll give you one simple opening question that will quickly engage your prospect and uncover what's on their mind, so you can press their mental "reset" button to ultimately gain their full attention.

Finally, I'll share the number-one takeaway I learned after a full year of high-level sales coaching. If you aren't already doing this, it will bring your sales results to an entirely different level by putting you solidly in control of the conversation.

WHAT HAPPENS BEFORE YOUR CALL MATTERS

When I started selling, I would often go through a ridiculous cycle of emotions: before the sales call, fear that I wouldn't close the deal. During the call, stressed-out hyper-self-awareness of what I was saying, because I didn't want to "screw up" the deal. This was followed by the intense hope I could get agreement to close the deal.

If the deal closed, I felt overwhelming relief. If I didn't close the deal, then frustration and negative self-talk kicked in: "What the heck, Brian—what was that? Are you kidding me? You just wasted that opportunity!" Then back to fear of not closing the deal when the cycle inevitably began again.

Selling is great, isn't it? Well, not like this it isn't.

When I stopped and paid attention to my internal dialog

prior to the sales call, here's what I realized: what I was saying to myself was, "Man, I hope I can get them interested and close a deal and don't screw up."

Ironically, what I found is that the fear of screwing up and not closing a deal was actually keeping me from closing deals. In a sense, thinking about those things became a self-fulfilling prophecy.

So instead of worrying about whether I'd make a sale, I focused my thoughts on becoming fascinated with my prospects as individuals and discovering their needs. As a result, my sales conversations and outcomes became dramatically more effective.

First becoming aware of what I was thinking and then proactively changing that pre-call mindset made a huge difference, because your prospect picks up on what's going on inside your head. They can feel it. And if someone senses your anxiety because you're only there to close a deal, it negatively affects the whole dynamic of the conversation. There's a higher probability that you will not close the deal.

So, I contemplated how I'd like to be treated by a salesperson and had a head-smacking moment: I would want that person to ask me intelligent questions, focus on my needs, have a conversation rather than a presentation, and be absolutely truthful about their product.

It's a state of serving the prospect instead of being self-serving.

I like what Ray Edwards says in his book *How to Write Copy That Sells*: "Our role is to help prospects make a decision—and it's either going to be 'Yes' or 'No.' You don't want to have the mindset of 'I have to sell you this' because the moment you do, you stop being interested in what's good for the prospect and ultimately become interested only in what's good for you."

PRE-CALL PREPARATION

I was listening to a podcast recently about the success habits of some of the best-performing athletes. What struck me about the commonality of these habits was that they all had a pre-game or in-game ritual. These were very specific things they did or thought that brought them into a state of peace and mental focus, so they could perform at their highest level.

What was especially interesting to me was the 10- to 15-second ritual of one of the world's top tennis players. Between each play, he would do several specific things that immediately lowered his heart rate and calmed his breathing so he could focus on the next ball. It was almost magical and had the ability to put him back into his highest and best state of performance every time.

What do you do before your sales calls to prepare yourself to connect with your prospect?

Our pre-call thoughts and rituals drive our actions and outcomes and can dramatically influence those of our prospect. Taking control of your pre-call thoughts and emotional state is crucial for success.

Often our assumptions and expectations about someone we're going to meet for the first time play out exactly as we've mentally conceived them. Not only that, your assumptions are "telegraphed" to your prospect and they will often rise—or fall, depending on your expectations—to that level by responding in the way you've imagined.

Before you ever meet your prospects, and regardless of the emotional state you may be in, choose in advance to care about and be fascinated with them as individuals.

It's no secret that people buy from those whom they like and trust, because trust is the foundation of all meaningful relationships.

Like your prospect first. Have that mindset and attitude when you walk in the door or pick up the phone for your appointment. If you like them first, you'll dramatically increase your chances of them liking and trusting you, which will set the stage for a great conversation.

SUGGESTED PRE-CALL RITUAL

Before your next sales conversation, pause and try the following:

Close your eyes, open your palms upward and take in a slow, deep breath, hold it for seven seconds, and slowly let it out, counting to seven again as you do so. Calm your mind, relax your body, and...comfortably smile.

Continuing to keep your eyes closed and palms up, take three or four slow, deep breaths in and out, while comfortably holding the smile on your face.

Now imagine speaking with the prospect and become grateful for them—truly grateful for the person you're about to speak with. Now verbalize your thankfulness for this person and choose to like and care about him or her in advance, no matter how they may respond.

Now pray for your prospect.

Pray they will be open to what you're going to communicate, and that you will be on the alert to respond to their needs and help them in any way possible.

Because, as I mentioned, whether you realize it or not, you are telegraphing and transmitting your heart to that person—even before a word is spoken.

I realize this may be totally out of your comfort zone, but I challenge you to try it before every sales conversation for one week. It only takes about 60 seconds.

Much like the professional tennis player I mentioned, after following this ritual for a long time, it now only takes me about 10 to 15 seconds to get into my pre-call mental and emotional state by thinking a few specific thoughts and saying a short, heartfelt prayer for my prospect.

Whether you follow the example I've given you or not, I highly recommend you make your own pre-call ritual. Be very purposeful about what you do and why you do it.

MATCHING AND MIRRORING

One of the most important secrets I discovered in rapport-building is the concept of matching and mirroring. Matching and mirroring a prospect physically will quickly build rapport. It will serve to eliminate the distance between you, create an unspoken bond, and ultimately build trust.

The first and most basic way to do this is by matching your prospect's posture. Is that person sitting rigidly upright? Slumped? Arms or legs crossed? Do the same thing.

You will better empathize with your prospect by matching their body language. When you mirror it, you are subconsciously telling them you are like them. People like people who are like them, so this creates rapport.

Second, you will want to mirror the prospect's speaking pace and volume. Don't worry if their volume seems unpleasant or the pace abrupt. Again, this will subconsciously tell your prospect you're like them and build an immediate bond of trust.

If I'm talking to someone in south Texas with a heavy drawl, I'll begin using it too. I'll say, "y'all" and use some of the same lingo. If I'm talking to someone in New Jersey, where people tend to speak more rapidly, I'll match and mirror that.

Third, if you want to connect with your prospect at an even deeper level, you can do so by adopting their breathing rhythm. Something powerful happens when you sync up your breathing pattern with another person's, as you are able to feel a little bit of whatever that person is feeling on a very physical level.

I begin just by observing the rise and fall of the prospect's chest, watching how they are inhaling and exhaling, and then matching it. I was astonished the first time I did this. I felt an amazing connection with my prospects. I was able to sense their energy and stress level, and this created a significant connection during the sales conversation.

Bear in mind that these various types of matching and mirroring techniques take practice. Take it one step at a time, rather than trying to duplicate everything at once.

When you start your conversation, just accept the prospect's body language, vocal pace, and breathing pattern and sync up with them.

Start first by making a goal of matching posture and body language. Do that one thing for a week. Then, when that becomes second nature to you, begin matching vocal pace and volume. Then match breathing. As you integrate this into your sales conversations, you'll be amazed how powerful it can be.

This becomes particularly effective when your conversation begins to move along and rapport gets stronger. Then you'll notice your prospect unconsciously beginning to match and mirror you!

This signals a shift, where you now have the ability to lead your prospect with your own enthusiasm and energy level. This is especially important when the conversation gets to the point of your educating them, and their body language and vocal pace reveal to you they trust and believe what you're saying.

For example, I've had many sales conversations where my prospect initially had a lackluster, kind of "meh" attitude. But as I matched and mirrored their behavior and continued talking, invariably things would begin to shift to where they started unconsciously mirroring and matching me. Then I was able to change the energy level and pace, and create excitement and enthusiasm for my solution.

However, if you don't sense they are matching you, it's OK. Just keep mirroring them, and your chances of developing a deeper connection will be greater than if you didn't do it at all.

At first, learning to match and mirror can be like learning to drive a car. Remember that? When you first learned, you were hyper-aware—conscious of your car being in your lane, other drivers, checking your speed, your blind spot, the mirrors, and the pressure of your foot on the accelerator. But now you drive on autopilot.

Just like any habit, it will take time for the action to become subconscious.

STARTING THE CONVERSATION

So, we've discussed the importance of having a great pre-call ritual and positive mindset, along with the power of matching and mirroring. Now, let's talk about one of the best conversation-starting questions I've ever discovered.

Before I share this, let me say I realize there are limitless ways to start a conversation with your prospect, such as: "Tell me how your [insert name of day] is going?" Or, "How about those [name of college or professional team that won]?" Or, "So, tell me, how's business been going?"

However, my favorite is this: "I'm curious. Have you had to put out any fires today?"

I found that asking this question is a great way to give your prospect permission to recognize and verbalize the reality of where their minds may be when you start the conversation.

What's more, getting their feelings out on the table will help them mentally set them aside for the time being, hit the "reset" button, and move into this moment where you're having a conversation with them.

Otherwise, you may be talking at them instead of with them, because their mind is somewhere else.

If they did have a fire to deal with, ask some appropriate questions about it. Have some dialogue. Find out what's going on to get it on the table. If they didn't just deal with some "fire," that's great. Tell them that since you asked, there's bound to be a fire now!

Usually, this won't take more than one or two minutes. You can then move into one of the most important moments in your sales conversation: setting the agenda.

SET THE AGENDA

One of the most dramatic increases in my sales occurred as a direct result of implementing a single idea I received during a year of professional sales coaching: setting an upfront agenda with each and every prospect.

When I began setting the agenda for my sales conversations, everything changed. The comfort level my prospects and I felt surged as a result of this new approach. It brought a higher level of confidence to my selling process and enhanced engagement for several reasons.

First, it creates open loops with your prospect by telling them what you're going to tell them. By doing this, they are going to anticipate the points of your agenda and will want to track with you along that path. It creates positive expectations.

By the way, an "open loop" is the concept that, when we promise something in the future, our minds want closure. For example, if you tell someone that you're going to show them a way they can double their productivity in 30 days, but first you want to give them some information about your company, their minds will be waiting for you to tell them how to double their productivity, and until you do, there's an open loop that needs to be closed.

Open loops are a very powerful means of creating engagement and anticipation.

Second, providing an upfront agenda boosts your prospect's confidence that you know where you're going, and it helps you stay on track with your sales process.

WHAT TO SAY

After connecting with your prospect, you simply transition to the agenda by saying, "Now, with your permission, what I'd like to do is share the agenda for our conversation. It's just three points. Is that OK?" Then share the points of your agenda.

A sample script is at the end of this chapter.

I've found this agenda-setting statement will immediately bring your prospect or an entire room full of people to attention, because you're about to tell them exactly where you're going with your conversation. It puts you in the driver's seat.

I cannot overemphasize how important this can be to your success in sales.

Moving from the rapport-building phase of the conversation to the sales conversation would often feel awkward and somewhat contrived. However, when I adopted the upfront agenda-setting approach, it gave me a rock-solid means of making that transition without grinding the gears, so to speak.

Here's an example script of how to set the agenda:

SAMPLE SCRIPT FOR
SETTING THE AGENDA

After your opening question and conversation, transition by saying this:

"Now, with your permission, what I'd like to do is share the agenda for our conversation. It's just three points. Is that OK?

"First, I'd like to ask you some questions about your business to get a better understanding of how you're marketing now.

"Second, if you're taking notes, I'm going to share the key components of our service with you.

"Third, I'd like to show you exactly how the service works, then we'll chat about pricing and finish up. OK?

"By the way, before we get started, let me share a little bit about our company..."

EXPLANATION

Let's look at the thought process behind each component of the agenda, and how you can customize it for your use.

"Now, with your permission, what I'd like to do is share the agenda for our conversation, it's just three points. Is that OK?"

Asking for **permission** is a softening statement that shows honor and respect for your prospect. You're **sharing** the agenda as opposed to "telling" them the agenda.

This is a three-point agenda. That's not random. We are hardwired to think in three's. A, B, C—1,2,3—Good, Better, Best. This creates an open loop for those points. We'll discuss more about the power of threes in Chapter 7, when we review pricing and guarantees.

"Is that OK?" could also be said, "Does that make sense?" or "Fair enough?" Whatever finisher you choose, you are reaching for an affirmative response.

> "First, I'd like to ask you some questions about your business to get a better understanding of how you're marketing now."

The first point let's your prospect know you're going to be asking some general questions about their current situation. Of course, this can be tailored to whatever you're selling. For example, let's say it's surveillance software: *"First, I'd like to ask you some questions about your current surveillance software and get a better understanding of how you're using it and where you'd like to see improvements."*

> "Second, if you're taking notes, I'm going to share the key components of our service with you."

"If you're taking notes" sets the expectation that your prospect will put pen to paper while you provide the overview of your product or service. You're essentially saying, "Hey, this is going to be important." It's a soft command that you'll come back to after the interview.

> "Third, I'd like to show you exactly how the service works, then we'll chat about pricing and finish up. OK?"

The third point sets up your conversation to educate and, as needed, demonstrate how your solution works. Then in an offhand manner, you say, **"...then we'll chat about pricing and finish up."** This creates an open loop to transition into pricing and an expectation that it will be a comfortable, non-threatening part of the conversation, because you're just going to **"chat"** about it. Then again, you're providing a finishing statement leading to an affirmative response and agreement by saying, **"OK?"**

> "By the way, before we get started, let me share a little bit about our company..."

This is a very important transition statement that helps answer the question, "Why should I listen to you?"

Because, that's exactly the question your prospect wants answered at the beginning of your sales conversation.

So, give them key reasons, like: "We've been in this space over 16 years and have more than 3,000 clients who have the exact business profile as you do." Or, "We are the number one provider of XY widgets in the world and have been given the President's award of distinction for widget innovation."

Next, we'll move into the all-important interview step. First, here's a summary of what we've covered:

CHAPTER SUMMARY

- Connecting with your prospect always starts before you enter their office or call them on the phone.
- Having a strong pre-call ritual will put you into the right mental and emotional state.
- The fear of not closing a deal will keep you from closing a deal.
- Become fascinated with your prospects as individuals and deeply desire to discover their needs.
- Your role is to help your prospect make a decision.
- Choose beforehand to like and care about your prospect.
- Calm yourself before your sales call with deep breathing—and smile!

- Be grateful for your prospect.
- Pray for your prospect.
- Match and mirror your prospect's:
  - Body language
  - Speaking pace and volume
  - Breathing
- Start your conversation by hitting the "reset" button for your prospect by asking if they've had to put out any fires today.
- Set the upfront agenda for every sales conversation.

CHAPTER 5

INTERVIEW

In this chapter, you're going to find out why you need to have a list of carefully crafted and sequenced questions you ask every prospect.

You'll learn how to create great questions, put them in the right order, and find out why you should always take notes on your prospect's answers.

Then I'll show you how to move from setting the agenda to the interview.

You'll also discover what "sales malpractice" is and how to avoid it.

THE KEY TO LIFE AND GREAT SALES

The questions you ask will make or break your selling career.

Questions are the absolute KEY to selling anything.

Without carefully crafted questions, I can promise that you will miss a multitude of opportunities to close sales, because you will not uncover all your prospect's deeper needs nor alert them to the other reasons they should purchase what you're offering.

The specific questions you ask, HOW you ask them, and the order in which they are asked will set up your conversation for success or failure.

I discovered this out of sheer necessity.

It happened when I was with Johnson & Johnson's Ethicon Endo-Surgery division. We sold disposable endoscopic and open-stapling devices—devices used along with a camera placed inside a patient and those used in "open belly" surgical procedures.

I was frustrated by the mediocre response I was getting to my line of questions about a new device we were promoting to general surgeons.

There was no doubt that our surgical device was clinically superior, but our competitor was entrenched in the space with a well-known product.

I just wanted to say to the surgeons, "Look, our device is superior. We have loads of clinical proof it's better than what you're using. So, you just need to try it."

End of story, right?

I wish.

I decided to sit down and do whatever it took to create the right questions that would bring the shortcomings of the competitive product to the forefront of my conversations.

But this had to be done in a way that won the surgeon over—that appealed to his heart and mind.

After hours of work, I finally had the list of about 10 questions. They went from general to specific, spoke to clinical benefits, and did so in a way that the surgeons could judge for themselves that our device was worthy of evaluation.

The results I experienced from asking specific questions in a specific order for a specific reason were immediate and dramatic.

Within 30 days, evaluations of my product doubled, and so did sales.

As I continued to update the questions and order in which they were asked, the results got better and better.

After that, whenever there was a new product release, the first thing I would do is look at its features, specific benefits, and the needs it would meet. Then I would start working on the questions.

As I trained other salespeople, they noticed I was working from a list of questions and would ask for a copy. When they used it, it worked for them as well. Eventually word spread around the sales organization and others started asking me for a copy of the "Robinson Question List."

The feedback was fantastic.

If the physician had an open mind, and the salesperson followed the questions in sequence, there was a high probability of success in gaining an evaluation of the device and closing the deal.

The questions you ask will directly determine the results you get.

Ask the same question—get the same results.

Ask a different question—get different results.

I cannot overemphasize how much your questions matter.

Gary Keller, in his book *The One Thing*, says, "...the quality of any answer is directly determined by the quality of the question. Ask the wrong question, get the wrong answer. Ask the right question, get the right answer. Ask the most powerful question possible, and the answer can be life altering."

I have a friend who is a top performer in a multilevel marketing business that sells essential oils. She created a specific script that includes carefully crafted questions she asks every prospect.

Her questions are so effective in moving prospects to action that other people in the organization are literally paying her thousands of dollars just to get a copy of them.

Those who carefully follow her script, asking the same questions, are experiencing incredible results.

HOW TO DEVELOP GREAT QUESTIONS

To develop great questions, follow this three-step process:

First, grab a piece of paper—or use a spreadsheet—and draw three columns. Label column one "features," column two "benefits," and column three "questions."

List a feature of your product or service in column one. Then, list all the corresponding benefits of that feature in column two.

Then, in column three, write out the question you can ask to reveal whether your prospect has a need for that benefit.

Repeat these steps for each feature of what you're selling, being as exhaustive as possible.

Keep in mind that most features will have several corresponding benefits. Also, most benefits will have several corresponding questions.

Let's look at a simple example of a feature-benefit-question series.

Let's say you're selling a digital video marketing service that's internet-based and allows your clients to update content on their in-lobby television screens within minutes.

FEATURE: Web-based content-management system

BENEFIT 1: Remotely update your in-lobby video content from anywhere in five minutes or less

BENEFIT 2: Schedule content changes any time in the future, on the day and time of your choosing

QUESTION 1: How long does it typically take you to update the content on your in-lobby televisions right now?

QUESTION 2: How far in advance do you now plan your video-content changes?

QUESTION 3: If you could plan your video content changes in advance and schedule them to start on a future date, how helpful would that be to your marketing efforts?

Bottom line: the questions you ask are meant to help your prospect think about what they're doing now, and spotlight the gap between what they're doing and what you offer. That's why your questions are the absolute key to selling anything.

Here's another example of a feature-benefit-question series.

Let's say you're selling pre-made home-cooked meals.

FEATURE: Pre-made home-cooked meals for two to six people

BENEFIT 1: Saves up to 60 minutes per meal, including food purchase, preparation, and cooking time

BENEFIT 2: Just pull it out of the freezer and put it in the oven

QUESTION 1: On a weekly basis, how many dinners do you cook for your family?

QUESTION 2: How much time does it typically take you to make a dinner for your family?

QUESTION 3: If you could just pull your dinner out of the freezer, already prepared, and put it into the oven without having to think about it, how would that affect the frequency of your family meals?

Next, order the questions from general to specific, placing the most compelling benefit questions first. In other words, think 80/20. What 20% of your benefits meet 80% of your customer or client needs? Put those questions at the top of your list, right after your general questions.

General questions are those that help you gather information to provide context for your discussion.

For example, if you were selling some type of advertising, general questions might include:

- So, help me understand: how do you currently market to your customers?
- What forms of advertising do you currently use? Social media, print, TV?
- Do you work with any third-party ad agencies to develop your advertising campaigns, or is all your creative work done in-house?
- What is it about your current work-flow or process you'd like to change or streamline if you could?

If you were selling zero-turn riding lawnmowers, examples of general questions might be:

- I'm curious: what type of lawnmower do you currently have?
- What's been your experience with that?
- How large is the area you're mowing and how long does it take to mow it now?
- Does your mowing area have trees, is it an open field, or a combination of both?

There's a compelling psychological benefit to asking carefully prepared questions. They give you a higher level of credibility because you are attempting to diagnose your prospect's problem or pain, just like a skilled physician probing a patient to find out where it hurts.

One of the greatest frustrations sales managers share with me is that their salespeople move way too quickly into presenting their solution, before getting an accurate diagnosis of the prospect's issues. In other words, they show up and throw up.

That's sales malpractice.

You cannot possibly provide a solution for your prospect's pain until you've performed a thorough diagnosis of their specific situation and have uncovered their needs. I am adamant when training sales people that, until you find a need, you cannot proceed to the solution.

In other words, you must earn the right to present your solution. And the only way you can do that is by asking questions that will provide you with the information you need to uncover a need. Otherwise, you're committing sales malpractice.

MOVING FROM SETTING THE AGENDA TO THE INTERVIEW

So, before you start asking questions, tell your prospect

that you have a list of questions and ask for permission to take notes about their answers.

I don't think I realized how truly compelling this was until a couple of years ago, when a friend of mine recommended I connect with a newly retired businessman in his early 50s.

I met him at a local coffee shop. When I joined him at the table, he already had a notepad and pen laid out. After a little chit-chat, he started asking questions about me and my work. He was genuinely interested.

He explained that he was getting bored with retirement after selling his medical-device business for several million dollars—poor fellow—and was now starting a new business in the disaster-recovery space. But what took me by surprise was that he was actually taking notes on my answers.

To be clear, this was not an interview. It was not a sales conversation. It was just a sit-down with somebody whom I'd never met. But the courtesy he showed in writing down the answers to my questions made me feel important. It made me want to give him more thoughtful responses, because I believed my answers mattered to him. As a result, I received a firsthand impression of just how valued that makes others feel.

When you are ready to start the interview, say this: **"I have a list of questions I've prepared and, with your permission, I'd like to take some notes on your answers. Is that OK?"**

At that point, open up your notepad—not your laptop—pull out your pen, and start asking your prepared questions in order. Underline, asterisk, or put a circle around any answer you want to refer back to when you present your solution. The clearer you are on your prospect's problem, the better you can address the solution.

If you do this, they will be more willing to reciprocate when you ask them to take notes on the key components of your product or service.

Also, this gives you a golden opportunity to capture your prospect's specific words and phrases, which you can refer to during the solution step of your conversation. It also provides you with a means to clarify and confirm what they've told you, because you can read back their own words.

Using your prospect's own words and phrases is a powerful feedback loop that brings deeper commitment and conviction to their own responses.

Dr. Robert B. Cialdini writes, in his book *Influence: The Psychology of Persuasion,* "...organizations have found that something special happens when people personally put their commitments on paper: They live up to what they have written down."

Wouldn't you agree that the next best thing is writing down your prospect's own words, then feeding them back to get confirmation? And when the time comes to refer to those answers, your prospect will tend to stay committed to what they've said, because you've confirmed it in their exact words.

This isn't some ploy to manipulate your prospect into a corner and use their words against them. It's actually a great way to bring honesty to the sales conversation and be sure you and your prospect are on the same page.

You'll then have the prospect's own words to use to frame your solution. How powerful is that?

By the way, after going through your list of questions, you might determine that one or more are not in the right order. Always be ready to reorder your list and place questions where they are most effective. The idea is to hit the high points faster and use the shortest route possible to uncover your prospect's needs.

"YOU'VE GOT 10 MINUTES—SHOW ME WHAT YOU'VE GOT AND HOW MUCH IT COSTS"

What do you do if you walk into your prospect's office for a scheduled appointment, start your conversation, and they look at their watch and say, "By the way, I only have about 10 minutes for you to give me your pitch."

I would first recommend that you try to reschedule the meeting then and there, without going any further. Sometimes this is just a tactic prospects use to see if it's worth spending additional time with you. If rescheduling isn't an option, then stick to your agenda.

Don't get knocked off your game. You came there to professionally diagnose their situation and see if there's a need for your product or service. So, as much as possible, stay focused on the diagnosis, even if you only have 10 minutes.

In this case, move forward by saying, "OK, I'm going to ask you some questions and then after 10 minutes, you can decide if we should continue our conversation or end it—fair enough?" Then pull out your phone or take off your watch, set it on the desk where both you and your prospect can see it, and start asking your most important questions.

What most salespeople do when only given a few minutes

to "make their pitch" is move into "fight or flight" mode and nervously begin to verbally vomit up all the reasons why people buy, or all their features and benefits, or jump to a demonstration, without ever having qualified the prospect.

Don't do it.

You must discipline yourself to stop and calmly ask questions that will determine if they qualify for what you're offering.

If you're prospect interrupts your questions with, "Look, I really don't have time for this, just tell me what it costs," pause and say, "Is price your only concern?" Most prospects will then stammer out something like, "Well no, it's not my ONLY concern, but it is important."

Then follow up with, "OK, I'm happy to share pricing options with you: which one would you like to know about?" They may say, "I don't know, what options do you have?" "Well, that's what I was going to discuss with you, but I've found that if I don't provide some context for pricing, the options won't make a lot of sense. So, I'd like to quickly provide you with some context first. May I do that?"

If your prospect still insists on the pricing options up front without giving you the courtesy of asking some qualifying questions, then, if you wish, give them a range: "It's between this and this. Do you want to continue the conversation or would you like me to stop here?"

The power of curiosity will usually prompt your prospect to say, "Let's continue."

I've only had one person ever stop me after asking that question. They had a dollar amount in mind that was much lower than my low-end pricing. No amount of persuasion was going to move them to a yes. But assuming the prospect allows you to keep going, then jump right back into your agenda and keep moving forward.

Bottom line: without a full understanding of the value provided by what you sell, the price for your offering will always seem "too high."

If you walked into any bank and wanted a loan for $50,000, they wouldn't just give it to you. They'd have to ask you questions—some very personal ones—to see if you *qualify* for the loan. The same holds true for your prospect. It's in their best interest and yours to see if they qualify for what you offer. And the only way to know is by asking intelligent questions to find out.

Next, we'll look at the most powerful methods you can use to present your solution. But first, here's a summary of what we've discussed in this chapter:

CHAPTER SUMMARY

- Questions will make or break your selling career.
- Have a list of carefully crafted questions you ask every prospect.
- Write out each feature, its corresponding benefits, and the questions that highlight those benefits.
- Order the questions from general, information-gathering questions to questions specifically related to the most important benefits your product or service provides. Think 80/20.
- You are attempting to diagnose your prospect's problem or pain, just like a skilled physician probing a patient to find out where it hurts.
- Until you find a need, you cannot proceed to the solution. If you do, that's sales malpractice.
- Ask for permission to take notes on the answers to your prospect's questions; then, actually take notes with pen and paper.
- Confirm your prospect's answers with their own words whenever possible, because this brings a deeper level of commitment to their stated needs.
- If your prospect says they only have 10 minutes, stick

with your agenda, focus on your preplanned questions, and stop the conversation at the 10-minute mark. Let them decide if you should move forward.

- Do not give pricing, even if your prospect demands it up front. Always attempt to provide context and only then provide a price range. It's always in your prospect's best interest and yours to see if they qualify for what you offer before quoting a price.

CHAPTER 6

PRESENT YOUR SOLUTION

In this chapter, you'll see how to transition from the interview to the overview and discussion of your solution.

You'll discover why directly telling your prospect what they should do will almost always work against you.

I'll show you the one attribute that all great sales people have in common, and how you can acquire it if you don't already have it.

Then we'll look at the difference between the Sales Talker and Sales Teacher, how many testimonials are "enough," and the best way to provide references when a prospect requests them.

THE OVERVIEW

After completing your interview questions, you will transition to an overview of your solution by saying the following: **"Now, if you've got a piece of paper handy, I'm going to have you list out the five moving parts of our service to give you an overview of what we offer."**

Obviously, you can customize this to your specific situation, such as, **"Now if you've got a piece of paper handy, I'll ask you to list the three key components of our solution."**

Providing an overview is essential because, like the upfront agenda, it sets up the next step of your conversation. It's an open loop in your prospect's mind that needs closure, so it creates engagement with what you're about to say.

What if you're selling something that has 10, 15, or 20 different points you want to highlight and you don't want your prospect to have to write down every single one? In that case, create a bullet-point list you can hand them as a reference sheet, so they can follow along with you. Then they can take notes on the sheet as you review it.

TAKING NOTES

You want your prospect to take notes for several reasons.

It helps them focus and pay closer attention to what you're saying, and is also proven to help transfer new information from short-term to long-term memory. Plus, it will make it a lot easier for you to refer back to a specific point if they've already noted it.

If they don't have a piece of paper and pen handy, always be ready to give them one. (Note: if your company provides swag like notebooks and pens, this is the perfect opportunity to get them to use it. You can then create mindshare as they continue to use the item with your logo on it.)

If you set the expectation of taking notes, they will. That expectation will also act as a psychological trigger for them to view you as an authority, because we take notes on what authorities tell us.

Then step through each key component of your offer. For example: "So, if you're taking notes, the first key component of our service is...The way this works is..."

Your prospect is taking notes on each point as you explain what it is and how it works, focusing your conversation on the areas where you uncovered their greatest needs during your interview.

Now, if you took good notes during your interview and

didn't commit sales malpractice by discussing your solution before uncovering a real need for your offer, you can repeat back to your prospect verbatim the frustration or problem they described, using their own words, as you step through each point.

However, rather than coming right out and saying, "Well, here are the frustrations and problems you mentioned, and this is my recommended solution," you educate them to a place where they recognize the need for your product or service, own that need, and lean forward into your solution.

This is the essence of professional selling.

You don't tell your prospect what they should do, but instead help them come to their own conclusions by guiding them to a place where they see, feel, and understand how your product or service is the answer to their problem.

You do that by using a very powerful tool that's proven to overcome resistance.

OVERCOMING RESISTANCE

If you go to a medical doctor, and are paying him to diagnose and give you advice and counsel for your problem, you'll listen to what he has to say and likely accept his recommendations.

If you've hired a life coach to help you move to the next level in your life and business, it's natural to accept and implement their recommendations to help you move forward.

On the other hand, because we are culturally conditioned not to trust salespeople whom we haven't paid for advice, there's going to be a natural resistance to their recommendations. Deep down, we don't necessarily believe they're working in our best interests.

So, if you directly tell your prospect that your product or service can do X, Y, or Z, or that it's the best option in the market, they will automatically resist what you're saying without even thinking about it.

You can overcome this conditioned resistance by educating your prospect with social proof.

In his book *Influence: The Psychology of Persuasion*, Dr. Robert Cialdini says, "The principle of social proof states that one means we use to determine what is correct is to find out what other people think is correct...We view behavior as more correct in a given situation to the degree that we see others performing it."

In other words, we look to those who have had firsthand experience with something we haven't tried as a means of guiding the correctness of our own decisions.

My definition of social proof in selling is: referring to the experience of others to validate the credibility of our recommendations.

The most powerful way to do this is through the use of stories.

As humans, we are hard-wired for stories. We speak in words, we think in pictures, and we learn from stories. Scientists have shown that storytelling affects our brain in several significant ways:

1. **Neural Coupling:** a story activates parts of the brain that allows listeners to turn the story into their own ideas and experience thanks to a process called neural coupling.
2. **Dopamine:** the brain releases dopamine into the system when it experiences an emotionally charged event, making it easier to remember, with greater accuracy.
3. **Mirroring:** listeners will not only experience similar brain activity to one other, but also to that of the speaker sharing the story.

4. **Cortex Activity:** when processing facts, two parts of the brain are activated: Broca's and Wernicke's areas. A well-told story can engage many additional areas, including the motor cortex, sensory cortex, and frontal cortex.

SOURCE: ONESPOT.COM

As you can see, our brains turn stories into **our own ideas and experience** through neural coupling, thus helping prospects to embrace your solution as **their** solution. Not only that, the stronger the emotions behind a story, the easier it will be to remember what you've said, with greater accuracy.

For your prospects to connect with your story, they must see themselves as participants in it. This is accomplished by telling them a relevant story of how one of their peers solved a problem by using your solution, and the positive outcome it had for them.

Think about this. Have you ever been to an event with a great speaker and afterward someone asks you what their message was? What you'll immediately recall is a powerful story you heard and how it made you feel, not the other 90% of the presentation. You may not even remember their name, but you'll remember their story.

Likewise, your prospects will connect with your stories

and how that made them feel long after the details of your product or service fade—which, by the way, will happen very quickly.

THE GOLF CLUB STORY

One day, out of the blue, I had a client in Kansas—who had been a subscriber to my on-hold message service for six years—call and tell me he wanted to cancel his agreement. My immediate response was to ask if we had dropped the ball or if there was a problem, but he said no. In fact, he thought our service was fantastic.

He just didn't think anyone was listening to the messages and didn't want to continue investing in something that he didn't think he was getting any value from. I told him I understood, and then asked if he would let me try an experiment before cancelling the service.

Every year, our company would sponsor a golf hole at various tournaments around the country and give away a driver worth about $300. I mentioned that I had an extra driver sitting in my office and that I'd like to give it away as a test of whether or not people were listening to the on-hold messages. I told him I would write five on-hold messages for him to use and would give away the driver to find out how many people would sign up for it. He said he'd give it a try.

For example, one of the scripts said, "We don't even know if you're listening to this, but if you are, please tell the receptionist you heard this message and you'll be entered into a drawing to win a free $300 golf driver."

What was the result?

In just 17 days, 97 people signed up to win the driver. Now, keep in mind, this happened with a client who didn't think anyone listened to messages while they were waiting on hold. He was shocked at the results. And yes, he kept our service.

I've shared this story countless times. In fact, this story alone was responsible for single-handedly eliminating virtually any concern in my prospect's mind about whether callers actually listen to on-hold messages and respond if given the right offer.

Because of this story, my prospects began to think about the possibilities of using our service in their businesses, where previously, they may had dismissed it as "elevator music" or "blah, blah, blah on hold."

Stories like this can unload your prospect's objections before they are ever brought up. The beauty of using a story is that the revelation of this benefit happens without you directly saying it. The story does the work for you.

So, tell stories that are related to the most important facets of your offer. But also be alert to emotional cues.

EMOTIONAL CUES

We tend to listen logically but buy emotionally. Even very analytical people will buy based on some level of emotion. There is a well-worn story from the real estate industry that emphasizes this point:

A real estate agent was walking a couple through a house, providing facts about square-footage, living spaces, and bedrooms. But when the agent walked the couple by a window, the woman who was seeing the house stopped and thoughtfully pointed out the cherry tree in the back yard, while mentioning that she also had one in her back yard as a child.

The agent wisely grabbed onto this seemingly insignificant bit of information.

As the tour continued, the agent made a point of noticing

the cherry tree, pointing out that you could see it from the kitchen and living-room windows, plucking that emotional string again and again, so to speak.

The couple eventually bought the house.

As a salesperson, that's what you also want to be tuned into. You want to be alert to see where the emotional resonance is and keep plucking that string.

That's why it's dangerous to go on autopilot when you're in a sales conversation. And when you have sold the same thing for a long time, there is a tendency just to go through the motions. If you do, you might miss the subtle responses your prospect has to the particular component of your product or service you should zero in on.

One more thought here. It's not enough to just share stories. You need to be fully engaged in your sales conversation with the mindset of being a teacher, because ultimately, that's how you want your prospect to view you.

ACCIDENTAL SUCCESS?

A friend of mine used to work for a well-known, world-class software firm. He was responsible for generating leads, which meant a lot of cold-calling. The company protocol required that after generating the lead, he would hand it off to a software expert, who would then come in and present solutions to close the deal.

Because he's passionate about technology, he wanted to learn all he could about the software. As a result, he "accidentally" started to close deals and became the top-performing salesperson in his company—without the software expert's assistance.

He didn't purposely try to do the software expert's job. This just happened as a natural outcome of answering his prospect's questions and teaching them about what his software could do for them.

The more you know about how your prospect can benefit from your product or service, and the more ways you can teach them about the specific value your solution brings through stories and other users' experiences, the more deals you're going to close.

That's why the best salespeople are the best teachers, and the best teachers lead their "students" to make their own conclusions with carefully crafted words, questions, and stories.

The best salespeople understand their product or service

so well that they know exactly what to give prospects to awaken their need for it. And even though they may have a library full of product knowledge, they provide only the most crucial information to help their prospect visualize the offer fitting perfectly as the solution to their problem.

Being a great teacher is more vital now than ever and will become even more significant in the future for two reasons: information overload and seemingly unlimited options for making a decision.

Because of that, prospects will reward you with their trust—assuming, of course, you have a worthy product or service—if you bring the most essential information for addressing their problem, issue, or pain, and show them the shortest path to the solution.

People purchase solutions only from people they trust.

As a master teacher, you wisely guide them to a place of awareness, citing best practices, testimonials, third-party references, and clinical proof wrapped in stories, so they embrace your solution, own it, and want to take action.

THE SALES TALKER VS. THE SALES TEACHER

What's the difference between how a typical salesperson—the Sales Talker—discusses their solution vs. the Sales Teacher? Here are some examples:

- **The Sales Talker:** "We know our service is superior to any other competitor in the marketplace."
- **The Sales Teacher:** "Every single client that has switched from a competitor to our service has told us, without question, that what we offer is superior to any other provider in the marketplace. In fact, we have over 97 testimonials on our website from clients who have confirmed this. For example, just last week I had a client in Tampa switch to us from competitor 'X' and they said they were astonished at how much easier it was to use our service."
- **The Sales Talker:** "People calling your business will love listening to our trivia messages while they are on hold, because they are engaging, lighthearted, and fun, and they're included at no extra cost with our service."
- **The Sales Teacher:** "I have clients call regularly to tell me that, if a customer is taken off hold during a trivia question, they'll ask to be put back on hold so they can hear the answer to the trivia question. For example, in Atlanta, we have a call center using our service that actually prints out the answers to the trivia questions and gives a copy to each call-center representative, so they're ready to share them with the customers who want the answer after being taken

off hold in the middle of a message! By the way, this feature is included free with our service."

Sales Talkers tend to speak in terms that are one-dimensional and fact-oriented, as opposed to three-dimensional and story-oriented.

Although these examples show that the same general idea is being communicated, the Sales Teacher will wrap the information in specific third-party references, testimonials, and clinical data to bring the idea to life and help the prospect see it from a "what other people just like you are doing," social-proof perspective.

GET TESTIMONIALS—LOTS OF THEM

You can never have too many testimonials; so, whatever you do, get them from your customers and get lots of them, because they're great social proof.

Virtually every prospect will have some reservations, questions, or concerns about moving forward with your solution. Testimonials are a wonderful way to show that the use of your product or service isn't really that risky, because so many others have already purchased it from you and succeeded as a result.

If you don't have many testimonials, here's a way you can get them quickly. In 48 hours, we received over 220 testimonials with a simple yet powerful incentive.

We sent out an email to our entire client base of more than 3,000 businesses, saying, "If you provide us with your testimonial about our service within the next 48 hours, you will be entered into a drawing to win one of ten $150.00 gift cards."

To make it simple, I created a template that our clients could complete with their own words, which became an idea-starter for them. Not only did we get flooded with testimonials, they were truly inspiring for our employees to read.

If a prospect is hesitating at the end of a sales conversation and not quite ready to move forward, I'll share the above story and offer to show them a special web page where we have all the testimonials posted.

Often, the prospects would just look at the sheer number of testimonials as they scrolled down the page, and without even reading any, turn to me and say, "This is really impressive. I'm ready to move forward."

WHEN SOMEONE ASKS FOR REFERENCES...

Often a prospect will ask whether you can give them references. You should have a printed list ready to give them, and also have at least two or three ready to call right there during a sales conversation. I'd say, "Yes, I have references. May I call a couple right now, so you can speak with them directly?"

As you can imagine, it's quite powerful to be able to pick up the phone when you're ready to close a deal and have one of your customers explain how your product or service has worked for them.

Not only does this close more deals for you, but it also reinforces the commitment of your own customer to the solution you've already sold them, since you're involving them in your sales process as a spokesperson.

In Chapter 7, we'll talk about how to present your pricing and guarantee(s). Before we do that, let's look at a summary of this chapter and some questions for your consideration.

CHAPTER SUMMARY

- After your interview, always transition to an overview of where you're going next before you present your solution.

- Always have your prospect take notes or have a bullet-point list you can hand them so they can follow along with you.
- Don't tell your prospect what they should do; instead, use third-party references and stories to help them come to their own conclusions by guiding them into a place where they see, feel, and understand how your product or service is the answer to their problem.
- Guard yourself against going on "autopilot" in your sales conversations by being alert to emotional cues.
- The best salespeople are the best teachers and make liberal use of social proof in the form of best practices, testimonials, third-party references, and clinical proof wrapped in story form.
- Sales Talkers use one-dimensional, self-focused, fact-oriented communication; Sales Teachers use three-dimensional, social-proof, story-oriented communication.
- Get as many testimonials as you can. They are the most powerful form of social proof.
- Have references ready who you can call when you're with a prospect.

QUESTIONS:

- How many testimonials do you have right now? How often do you refer to them? What could you do to get more of them?
- What stories do you currently use to sell your product or service? How could you develop more real-world stories and integrate them into your sales conversations?
- How would you characterize your selling style right now? Are you a Sales Talker, a Sales Teacher, or a mixture of both?
- If you could change one thing right now about your sales conversation, what would it be?

CHAPTER 7

YOUR PRICING AND GUARANTEES

After the presentation of your solution, it's time to reveal your pricing and guarantees.

In this chapter, we'll discuss:

- The power of threes and why this matters in your pricing
- How the power of threes can help with your negotiating
- Why you should reveal your pricing from highest to lowest and not the other way around
- Why you should always offer a guarantee or set of guarantees
- What you can guarantee

- How offering unique guarantees doubled sales for one of my consulting clients
- A sample script of how to transition into a pricing discussion after presenting your solution

PRICING LESSONS

There are countless articles, studies, books, and blogs that have been written about pricing and pricing strategies.

What I'm going to give you is my best "real world" recommendation for pricing, based upon years of testing and tweaking pricing scenarios with prospects all over the United States.

Depending on what you sell, this may work perfectly for you. If not, it's the underlying concept that should be considered. Obviously, there's no "one size fits all" pricing scenario. However, this pricing approach helped my prospects quickly and easily understand their options, so they could make a great decision.

The first and most important lesson relates to the power of three. We all like to have choices, yet we tend to prefer choices that are limited to a few options. I've found that three options are instantly and intuitively understood. Two options are too few and four options are too many.

What's so magical about three? Well, it seems to be a universal theme that has built-in resonance. There's a beginning, middle, and end. Water is liquid, vapor, and solid. We are three-part beings: body, mind, and spirit. 1, 2, 3—A, B, C—Gold, Silver, Platinum—Good, Better, Best. There's completeness about the number three.

When I began selling on-hold messages, we had one price point for the service. And while that price was fine for some prospects, others asked if they could reduce the price by eliminating options they didn't feel were necessary, or changing terms or payment options. Those questions kept arising, and I had to negotiate a lot of custom, one-off deals.

So, I began to test different packages and pricing, eventually landing on the one that proved superior to the others. It had three options: A, B, and C. Option A was Premium, B was Midpoint, and C was Basic. As a result, closing deals became a whole lot easier.

The second lesson I learned is that when you move from a single price point to three pricing options, the decision is no longer yes or no. The decision now becomes, which one?

It became so much easier to close a deal. And the added

benefit was that if someone was hesitating between option A and B, or B and C, I had the flexibility to craft a deal in-between those options. It was a win-win. That wouldn't have happened nearly as easily with a single price point.

TRANSITIONING INTO THE PRICING DISCUSSION

After presenting your solution, you transition into your pricing discussion by saying, **"Okay, let's chat about pricing. It's very simple. If you're taking notes, there are three options: A, B, and C. Option A is our Unlimited program with unlimited changes** [and whatever other features are included], **Option B is our Midpoint program that gives you..., and Option C is our basic program that includes..."**

The key takeaway here is to explain the differences between the options, but not to reveal pricing just yet. You'll do that in a moment. By doing this, you're helping your prospect focus on which solution would be the best fit for them without the added consideration of pricing.

After presenting your options, tell your prospect what percentage of your customers choose which option—social proof—and ask which one they'd like to try. For example: **"My experience is that about 70% of our customers** choose Option A or B because of the flexibility it offers, and about 30% choose Option C. Now, if you were to give this a try, which option do you think might make the most sense to consider?"

By telling them what "most" customers choose, then asking which option they'd like to try, they are making a choice based upon the merits of each option you've described, as opposed to price.

When you tell them what percentage of your customers choose which options, you are using social proof to help your prospect see the correctness of their potential decision.

They may be thinking: "I'm interested in Option B and 70% of other buyers purchase either A or B, so it sounds like I'm in the right spot with my thinking."

As mentioned in Chapter 6, my definition of social proof in selling is: referring to the experience of others to validate the credibility of our recommendations.

By asking, **"Now, if you were to give this a try, which option do you think might make the most sense to consider?"** you're giving your prospects the freedom to share their thoughts without having to make a commitment. The key words here are "if" and "consider," neither of which indicate they are making a commitment. This is a great trial-closing approach to warm prospects up to making a decision.

Again, keep in mind this conversation is happening before you've given your prospect the pricing.

PRESENTING YOUR TERMS AND PRICING

Next, set up your pricing by explaining how your customers typically pay for your product or service. Knowing that the majority of your clients choose a specific term raises their comfort level.

For example: **"Now, here's the bottom line: 95 to 96% of our clients are on a 36-month term with us, because it's the best pricing. We offer shorter terms, but the pricing is significantly higher. So, that's why the vast majority of our clients choose a 36-month term.**

"Option A, the Unlimited program, is $199/month; Option B, the Midpoint program, is $159/month; and Option C, the Basic program, is $129/month. Does that make sense?"

Present your highest-priced option first because of the

concept of anchoring. A product or service isn't necessarily "cheap" or "expensive," it's relative to the value you've created.

People automatically look for some point of comparison when assigning value to a product or service, so if you begin with the highest-priced option as the point of reference—the anchor—the other options will look comparatively less expensive and therefore potentially more attractive.

By having three price options, you're essentially creating a high and a low anchor, Options A and C, which will typically move your prospect to choose Option B in the middle.

After presenting the pricing, you then share your guarantee(s). I'll give you a script for that in a moment.

THE GUARANTEE

Besides the quality of your product or service and the testimonials of your customers, your guarantee may be the single most important piece of your sales conversation, because it reverses the risk of purchase away from your prospect, so that they can confidently say yes to your offer.

A great guarantee has the potential to dramatically set you

apart from your competitors, even if you offer a similar product or service.

All things being equal, the one who has the best guarantee will win the sale.

You can guarantee virtually anything and should consider every possibility when crafting your guarantees.

For example, I consulted with a company in Colorado that was trying to increase sales for their loan-processing software to banks and credit unions. This software could take what would normally be five to six days of work, with multiple employees needed to pull and assemble loan documentation to prepare for an external audit, and reduce it to less than 60 minutes.

The software also virtually eliminated the possibility of missing documentation, which so often plagued the loan process.

Of course, other companies were offering this type of software, so they weren't the only ones operating in the market.

I asked what type of guarantees the other companies offered. For instance, was anyone guaranteeing audit-preparedness within an hour? It turned out nobody was.

We ended up offering four guarantees, each of which had a dollar amount associated with it. In other words, if the company couldn't make good on one of the guarantees, it would have to pay the customer a penalty—a hefty penalty!

One of the guarantees was that if the prospect was not fully prepared for an audit within 49 minutes or less, the company would pay them $5,000. Another guarantee promised zero-exception reports, which would really be going out on a limb in the old manual loan processing system. For every exception report that did occur, the company would shell out $200.

The four guarantees spoke to the major frustrations that every bank and credit union experienced when preparing for an audit. So, to create massive interest at the beginning of their sales conversations—even before they talked about any of the details of their software—I had the sales reps open up their presentations with their four guarantees.

After that, their sales more than doubled.

Was their software twice as good as their closest competitor's? No. It was nearly the same. But their closest competitor didn't offer any of these guarantees.

The point is that the right guarantees can set you head

and shoulders above your competitors and get more deals closed for you, even if you offer the same thing.

One of the most interesting truths I've discovered about guarantees—and you should test this for yourself—is that the longer the guarantee, the fewer returns you'll get or refunds you'll need to make.

For example, I used to offer a 30-day money-back guarantee on my service. The cancellations and refunds would be several per year.

I then offered a 90-day money-back guarantee, and cancellations and refunds dropped in half.

Then I offered a 90-day money-back guarantee, and the right to cancel the service any time in the first 12 months with a prorated refund. You know what happened? My cancellations and refunds dropped to near zero.

Did the service change? No. Only the guarantees changed.

A longer guarantee period takes the pressure off your buyer, so the perceived risk is less, as opposed to a shorter guarantee period, where the perceived risk is more.

So, I encourage you to test longer guarantees and see what this does for your sales.

WHAT CAN YOU GUARANTEE?

You can guarantee just about anything—satisfaction, terms, delivery, customer service, ease of use, performance, whatever.

Below are some examples as idea-starters:

- 90-Day Money-Back Guarantee
- 12-Month Money-Back Guarantee
- Unconditional Money-Back Guarantee
- No-Questions-Asked Anytime Refund
- Be Up and Running in Five Minutes or It's FREE
- Delivered in 30 Minutes or It's FREE
- 24-Hour Replacement-Service Guarantee
- 30-Day Test-Drive Guarantee
- Be Ready for an Audit in Less Than 49 Minutes or We'll Pay You $5,000
- Double Your Sales Leads or the Service Is FREE
- Price-Match Guarantee
- Double Your Money-Back Guarantee
- No Quibble, No Hassle, No Worries, Unconditional 180-Day Money-Back Guarantee
- If We Repair It and It Happens Again within 12 Months,

We'll Fix It for FREE and Give You a No-Questions-Asked 100% Refund Just for the Hassle
- After the First Half Day of the Conference, If You Don't Think You've Received $2,000 in Value, We'll Refund Your Money and Pay for Your Hotel Stay
- If You Find Any Other Vendor Who Can Offer the Same Features We Do, We'll Give You a $250 Visa® Gift Card Just for Telling Us about It.
- If Anything Ever Happens to Your Furniture, We Will Fix It at No Cost. Forever.

OPTIONS—PRICING—GUARANTEE

Here's the complete script for reviewing options, pricing, and including guarantees.

OPTIONS—PRICING—GUARANTEE SCRIPT

"Okay, let's chat about pricing. It's very simple. If you're taking notes, there are three options: A, B, and C.

"Option A is our Unlimited program with...; Option B, the Midpoint program, gives you...; and Option C is our basic option with...

"My experience is that about 70% of our customers choose Option A or B because of the flexibility it offers, and about 30% choose Option C. Now, if you were to give this a try, which option do you think might make the most sense to consider?"

Wait for your prospect's reply.

"OK, so, here's the bottom line: 95 to 96% of our clients are on a 36-month term with us, because it's the best pricing. We offer shorter terms, but the pricing is significantly higher. So, that's why the vast majority of our clients choose a 36-month term.

"Option A, the Unlimited program, is $199/month; Option B, the mid-point program, is $159/month; and Option C, the basic program, is $129/month. Does that make sense?

"Now, there are two guarantees we offer with our service. The first is a 90-day, 100% money-back guarantee. Then, we give you the right to cancel our service anytime in the first 12 months with a prorated refund.

"For example, you could go 10 months down the road with our service, cancel it, and we'll give you a full refund of the remaining months that you prepaid. I don't know of any other vendor that even offers that.

"Now, as you look at each option—A, B, or C—which one do you think might make the most sense to try?"

WHAT IF YOU DON'T HAVE THE AUTHORITY TO CREATE UNIQUE GUARANTEES?

Craft the best guarantees that you believe would help you close more deals. If your prospect is hesitating, ask an "if I could" question: "If I could provide you with a guarantee of X, would I be able to earn your business today?" If they say yes, then call your manager and let him or her know that if they could make that concession, you could get the deal. Let your manager make the commitment or bring it up the chain of command to consider. You will never know unless you try.

The other option would be to ask if you could test-market a certain guarantee or set of guarantees to prove their validity and ability to help get deals closed. Nothing ventured, nothing gained. What have you got to lose?

WHAT IF THREE PRICE POINTS DON'T MAKE SENSE FOR YOUR PRODUCT OR SERVICE?

What if you offer custom solutions and don't have the ability to provide three clear-cut options? I would suggest you look at your current clients from an 80/20 perspective. For example, what do 80% of your clients tend to include in your custom solution? Reference these key components, then create a general package that gives your client the ability to choose an A, B, or C option for the remaining 20%, based on additional features.

CHAPTER SUMMARY

- Present your options first.
- Reference what other customers typically choose.
- Ask what your prospect would choose "if" they were to give it a try.
- Reference what other customers choose as their typical term.
- Present your pricing for each option without asking for a commitment yet.
- Present your guarantee(s).
- Ask which option the prospect would like to try.
- You can guarantee almost anything.
- Have multiple guarantees.
- Make your guarantees as long as possible to reduce perceived risk.

In the next chapter, we'll demystify the all-important step of closing the deal.

CHAPTER 8

CLOSE THE DEAL

In straight-commission sales, if you walk out the door without getting a deal, there's a 90% chance you will not get a deal with that prospect the following week, month, or even next year.

You lose and your prospect loses. Unfortunately, it happens far too often.

In this chapter, we'll discuss:

- What closing is
- Why you should always have a deadline with a special offer
- How to present your special offer with your pricing
- How to introduce a one-time incentive to get a deal closed

- Why "I have to think it over" is the same as getting a no, and what to do about it
- How to quit chasing your prospects for an answer once and for all
- How to get prospects who are ignoring you to respond almost immediately
- Why your prospect's fear of loss is your greatest opportunity to close a deal
- How you can double your closing ratio with one simple question

WHAT IS CLOSING?

Closing is asking for the business and getting your prospect's authorization to move forward.

It's not some magical or mystical moment in the sales conversation where all the stars align, the angelic hosts begin to sing, and the prospect—in some hypnotic state—grabs your pen and signs the deal, while you're secretly hoping you can get out of their office before they "wake up" and realize what they've just done.

It's no secret why you're there in the first place. You're there to sell something. Your prospect is expecting you to ask for their business. So, ask for it.

Though we'd like to believe people will purchase strictly on the merits of our product or service, you have to be prepared to overcome their natural fear of parting with their money. Often, it will take just a little added encouragement to make this happen.

That's why you should always be ready with a special offer and deadline, or the ability to negotiate a special incentive at the time of closing.

When I first began selling, I would get to the end of the conversation with my prospect, ask for a decision, and then often hear, "Well...let me think about it. Can you call me back next week?"

Instead of pressing for their real objection about what they had to "think about," I'd say, "OK, I'll call you next week." Then I'd pack up my stuff, shake their hand, leave my business card, and walk out the door.

However, when I did this I felt relieved and deeply conflicted at the same time. Relieved because their answer wasn't a flat out no, so there was some glimmer of hope they might say yes. Conflicted, because I knew they were essentially telling me no, and that asking me to call back next week was their way of ending the conversation without actually telling me the answer was no.

I would walk out the door with this gnawing awareness that I was leaving a deal on the table, but wasn't sure how to get it closed. Definitely not a good place to be if you want to improve your selling.

Invariably, I would call back and they would tell me to call again in another week, or simply ignore my follow-up calls, voicemails, and emails.

In reality, the deal was dead, but I played the hope game with myself.

We've all done it.

The hope game is where you look at your call-back list and think: "If I can just get some of these deals to close I'll have a great month, so I'm going to keep reaching out to them and hopefully someone will move forward"—even though they've been ignoring your repeated attempts to contact them the past 30, 60, or 90 days.

Hello? Hope is not a strategy—especially in sales.

The truth is that without gaining a commitment from your prospect for the next action—any action—your deal might as well be dead the moment you walk out the door or hang up the phone.

Setting the appointment, driving hundreds of miles to get there, spending the previous night in a hotel away from your family—all of it wasted.

HOW DO YOU FIX THIS?

There's definitely a way to increase the odds of closing a deal. It's going to require some courage and uncomfortable conversations, but it'll be worth it.

Here's what I discovered:

First, a "maybe" or "I have to think it over" might as well be a no. You have to commit to getting a yes or a no before leaving your prospect's office.

Second, if you can't get the deal signed then and there, then you need a specific follow-up appointment booked in both your calendar and the prospect's before leaving. A "call me back next week" isn't good enough. What day and time are you both going to agree to speak again, and why?

If the prospect isn't willing to calendar a specific day and time for a follow-up call, and says, "Oh, just call me anytime next week, I should be available," then press them by saying: "I'm just wondering: do you not want to set a specific follow-up time because you're not really interested in moving forward, or is there some other concern?"

That question became an immediate difference-maker, because my prospect would often share their concern or objection, which I could then address.

This gave me the opportunity to then ask if there was anything else they had questions about and to try to close the deal. It also gave them the freedom to tell me no, so we didn't wind up wasting each other's time with worthless follow-ups.

The best time to address the concerns of your prospect is while you're with them. Not next week, when they've forgotten everything about what you're selling.

Assuming you've done your job asking great questions, uncovering their needs, and showing the value of your solution in meeting those needs, you owe it to yourself and your prospect to get them to say yes or no to your offering before you walk out the door or hang up the phone.

If there's a legitimate reason for them not to give you a definite yes or no answer while you're there, then you must schedule a specific follow-up appointment for the next step. Life is too short to waste your time chasing prospects that have already decided against your offering, but are too afraid of perceived conflict to let you know that up front.

Of course, sometimes multiple presentations are necessary to get a deal done. If someone else has to be involved in the decision process, perhaps a committee or executive team, then a follow-up appointment is going to be appropriate. Always have a next step planned. That's the bottom line.

Hope is never a strategy for getting sales. Getting a yes, no, or calendaring the next step is the only strategy that will help you and your prospect move forward.

MY PROSPECT IS JUST IGNORING ME NOW

There's a saying with dentists: if you ignore your teeth long enough, they'll go away. The same holds true in selling. If your prospect ignores you long enough, they hope you'll just go away.

Do you have a hope list of prospects you've been chasing for months? Get back your self-respect and the personal power you've given to your prospects, and do this immediately: contact every one of them and get a yes or no.

I have a friend who was in the insurance industry and had

been chasing prospects month after month. He was sick and tired of it. In fact, he was so sick and tired of it, he was planning to quit his insurance business.

So, he decided that he was going to call every single one of the prospects on his hope list and get them to say no. He wasn't even trying to get them to say yes. He just wanted to prove to himself that all his deals were dead and that it was time for him to quit the insurance business.

As he called each one on the list he said, "I'm just calling to confirm that you're not moving forward with the insurance we discussed—that it's over."

With each person he crossed off his list, he felt more and more clarity, confidence, and self-respect. A funny thing started happening though: some of the prospects he called said they were going to move forward and were ready to sign a deal.

He broke his quota for the month, wound up staying in the insurance business, and eventually went on to become the top producer in the country!

There's some powerful psychology going on here. Many of our prospects, when confronted with the potential of the sales relationship ending or "being over," will move to make a decision.

I've seen this play out many times and have a specific email I send to those prospects who have stopped responding to me.

> Subject: [Prospect's First Name]—Is it "Dead" or "Alive?"
>
> Dear [First Name],
>
> I've attempted to connect with you via phone and email and unfortunately haven't received any response. So, I'm just curious: is it "Dead" or "Alive?"
>
> Thanks for letting me know one way or another if you'd like me to make any further contact or if I should go ahead and close your file.
>
> Either way, I look forward to the courtesy of your reply.
>
> Best regards,

At least 80% of the time, I will receive a response, often within minutes of sending the email. I've had many people reply, "Please don't close my file, we are definitely interested." which allows me to move things forward.

I've also had prospects say, "I'm so sorry for not responding. Unfortunately, we are not interested at this time." OK, great. Cross them off your list and move on.

THE SPECIAL OFFER AND FEAR OF LOSS

A special offer is a temporary offer with a deadline that gives your prospect the opportunity to get special pricing, terms, an enhanced guarantee, or any kind of "kicker" that gets them to do business with you now, as opposed to later.

What will your prospect lose by not doing business with you? How can you make that potential loss even greater with some special offer they have to act on now?

The more acute the potential for pain—or in the case of your prospect, fear of loss—the greater the motivation to avoid it. That's why having a special offer is so important in getting a deal closed.

Studies show people are twice as likely to take action to avoid pain or loss as they are to obtain pleasure or gain. In other words, if someone is doing well and you offer them a means of doing even better, they are less likely to take advantage of your offer than if you tell them what they'll lose by not doing so.

By the way, a special offer isn't "special" unless it has a deadline that creates urgency.

Plus, having a deadline legitimizes your reason to follow

up with your prospects if they don't move forward with your offer at the time of your initial sales conversation.

Think about it. If you walk out of a prospect's office with a follow-up appointment set for next week, how likely are they to keep that appointment or reply to your follow-up attempts if they don't have something to lose by not taking action by a specific date?

What if it were you? How likely would you be to respond to a salesperson who was following up with you, and you had no deadline for making a decision on their offer?

As Kevin O'Leary would say in the reality TV show *Shark Tank*, "You're dead to me." That's what your prospect is "saying" to you if you don't have a deadline.

Now, do you absolutely need special offers or incentives? No. Not unless you want to dramatically increase your odds of closing a deal.

For example, I was working with a prospect who was using a direct competitor of ours. I initially gave them a free two-week trial on our service, which went well. However, the deal just sat there for over 30 days after the trial period, because they were in the midst of several major projects. I scheduled a follow-up call with the decision makers and provided a special incentive on my pricing with a deadline.

Also, the primary decision maker was in and out of the office because of family health issues she had to attend to. So, 48 hours before the deadline, I had a legitimate reason to provide a "friendly reminder" that the special pricing and deadline were going to expire. This immediately put my offer at the top of her priority list, and within 24 hours I had a signed contract in hand.

If I didn't provide the special pricing offer and deadline, that deal never would have happened.

PRESENTING YOUR SPECIAL OFFER—SAMPLE SCRIPT

How do you present a special offer? Do it *before* you reveal your pricing. Here's a sample script using the pricing discussion from chapter 7 and inserting the special offer, which is underlined.

PRESENTING YOUR SPECIAL OFFER SCRIPT

"Okay, let's chat about pricing. It's very simple. If you're taking notes, there are three options: A, B, and C.

"Option A is our Unlimited program with...; Option B, the Midpoint program, gives you...; and Option C is our Basic option with...

"My experience is that about 70% of our customers choose Option A or B because of the flexibility it offers, and about 30% choose Option C. Now, if you were to give this a try, which option do you think might make the most sense for you to consider?

"OK, now here's the bottom line: 95 to 96% of our clients are on a 36-month term with us, because it's the best pricing. We offer shorter terms, but the pricing is significantly higher. So, that's why the vast majority of our clients choose a 36-month term.

"We have a special promotion running through [date] that provides a great discount off the rates I'm going to share with you after I present our pricing.

"Option A, the Unlimited program, is $199/month; Option B, the Midpoint program, is $159/month; and Option C, the Basic program, is $129/month. Does that make sense?

"Now, there are two guarantees we offer with our service. The first is a 90-day, 100% money-back guarantee. Then, we give you the right to cancel our service anytime in the first 12 months with a prorated refund.

> "For example, you could go 10 months down the road with our service, cancel it, and we'll give you a full refund of the remaining months that you prepaid. I don't know of any other vendor that even offers that.
>
> *"Here are the additional discounts we're offering on our service: if we earn your business by [date], the Option A price goes from $199/month to [discount rate], Option B goes from $159/month to [discount rate], and Option C from $129/month to [discount rate].*
>
> "Now, as you look at each option, A, B, or C, which one do you think might make the most sense to try?"

By preempting your price with the information that there is a special promotion, you once again create an open loop that your prospect will expect you to close with the special offer.

THE POWER OF ASKING

Although special offers are powerful motivators to get deals closed, providing one-time incentives can be just as powerful, if you ask.

Closing is, after all, asking for the business. You are asking your prospect to make a promise to pay you for goods delivered or services rendered. An incentive is just a way to sweeten or seal the deal, but you still need to ask. And if you doubt the power of simply asking for something, consider the following:

I have a friend who owns and operates a couple Chick-Fil-A restaurants in Tulsa, Oklahoma. He was planning a trip to Maui for a big event and was interested in doing a little experiment. He wanted to prove to himself that if he just asked people for money, he could fund his trip without paying for it.

It wasn't a question of money, because he had plenty. He just wanted to see what would happen if he asked for it.

He started asking his friends this question: "I am going to a conference in Maui. I can pay for it, but I wanted to know if you would be open to giving me just $25 toward it?"

People started opening up their wallets. He got almost the whole trip paid for just by asking other people if they would help him, even though he told them he could pay for it.

You won't know unless you ask the question. So why not ask it?

HOW TO DOUBLE YOUR CLOSING RATIO

One of the most powerful questions you can ask to open

up a conversation regarding an incentive is the "If I could, would you" question:

"**If I could** provide some incentive for you to move forward now as opposed to later, **would you** be open to hearing about it?"

The beauty of this question is that you're only asking **permission** to talk about an incentive. Your prospect gets to choose whether you have that discussion.

Virtually 100% of the time, they will want to know what incentive you're thinking of offering, because they are wondering what they might lose if they don't take advantage of it.

Then you ask the "if I could, would you" question again and just fill in the blank with your incentive: "If I could give you free installation and a month of free service?" "If I could give you the second setup free?" "If I could waive this fee or that, would you be open to moving forward now?"

Using that one question literally doubled my closing ratio.

You can also soften this question a little by adding the words "I'm just curious" or, "I'm just wondering" at the beginning.

For example, "I'm just curious: if I could provide some incentive for you to move forward now as opposed to later, would you be open to hearing about it?"

I provide many more examples of these proven "power phrases" in Chapter 11.

COMBINING YOUR SPECIAL OFFER AND INCENTIVE

Sometimes a special offer isn't enough to get a deal done. Perhaps your prospect has an existing agreement that needs to be addressed, because they will lose their investment in that product or service by switching to your offer.

In that case, you may need to provide both a special offer and a onetime incentive to potentially "buy out" your prospect's current agreement or investment.

That's when you want to be prepared to offer an incentive on top of your special offer.

CHAPTER SUMMARY

- Closing is not some mystical moment in the sales conversation. It's asking for the business and getting your prospect's authorization to move forward.

- Your prospect is expecting you to ask for their business. Hint: they know why you're there.
- Always be ready with a special offer and deadline, or the ability to negotiate a special incentive at the time of closing.
- Stop playing the hope game and get your prospect to give you a yes a no, or a definite next step. It will give you back your confidence, clarity, and self-respect.
- Getting a "maybe" or "I have to think it over" is the same as getting a no. Find out why your prospect is giving you this answer.
- The best time to address your prospect's concerns is while you're with them. Not next week, when they've forgotten everything about what you're selling.
- Tell your prospect that you have a special offer with a deadline before you present your pricing. This creates anticipation and fear of loss—what your prospect may lose if they don't take advantage of your special offer.
- Do not be afraid to ask a prospect who may be hesitating to sign a deal: if you could provide some incentive to move forward now as opposed to later, would they be willing to talk about it?

QUESTIONS:

- Are you happy with the amount of business you're closing?
- What one thing could you start doing now that would help you close more business?
- Do you have a special offer with a deadline? If not, what offer could you create to instill a sense of urgency with your prospects?
- What incentive could you provide to motivate your prospect to act now as opposed to later?
- Are you chasing your prospects for an answer? Why?
- What could you do today so you won't have to chase your prospects tomorrow?

CHAPTER 9

TOP SELLING CHALLENGES AND HOW TO OVERCOME THEM

1. LOSING A DEAL THAT YOU FELT CERTAIN YOU WOULD CLOSE

Nothing in sales can be more crushing than losing a deal that you thought you had locked up. All the signals were positive, but, in the end, you didn't get the business.

While most salespeople will just move on to the next opportunity, the most important thing you can do is find out why you lost the deal and learn from that.

If there is a silver lining to not closing a deal, this is it. And you can use it to fail forward.

You now have an opportunity to gain some priceless feedback that can help you win next time.

So, the next time you lose a deal, reach back out to your prospect and ask this question, "We are always looking to improve, so for my notes—I'm just curious—why did you decide to go with [vendor name]?"

Most prospects are fine with telling you their reasoning, and some aren't. In some cases, you might be surprised to learn they misunderstood your offer and that, in fact, you do have a better solution. You may even be able to restart the dialogue and save the deal.

Feedback is the food of champions. So, get that feedback as often as you can.

2. YOUR PROSPECT HAS STOPPED RESPONDING TO YOU

It's frustrating when you leave voice messages and emails but don't hear back from your prospect. If that's happening to you, re-read the chapter on closing, and use the proven "Is it dead or alive?" email script.

As mentioned, I've experienced at least an 80% response rate when using this email template:

> Subj: [First Name], Is it "Dead" or "Alive?"
>
> Dear [First Name],
>
> I've attempted to connect with you via phone and email and unfortunately, haven't received any response. So, I'm just curious, is it "Dead" or "Alive?"
>
> Thanks for letting me know one way or another if you'd like me to make any further contact, or if I should go ahead and close your file.
>
> Either way, I look forward to the courtesy of your reply.
>
> Best regards,

Oddly enough, there is something liberating about closing someone's file. Doing so frees up your mental and emotional bandwidth and allows you to focus on serious prospects. It also allows you a degree of pride, in that you're not going to keep chasing this person like a lost puppy. You have better things to do with your time.

Then, there's the added bonus that every once in a while, the threat of closing the file on someone lights a fire under them, and you wind up closing a deal instead of a file.

3. YOU'RE STRESSED OUT, EXHAUSTED, AND OVERWHELMED

Whenever you get totally worn down, you have to rest. It's just that simple. Unplug. I don't care how busy you are or how hectic things get. You have to stop what you're doing, shut off your phone, and give yourself permission to take a break.

Sometimes, just a 15- or 20-minute break is enough time to restore your poise and reduce your anxiety.

It's a common but mistaken belief to equate frenetic activity with success. It's focused activity that will bring you success, not activity for the sake of activity, just to make you feel like you're somehow being productive. You are simply on a hamster wheel running fast but getting nowhere. You can keep moving, but you're just wasting time and energy.

If you're not 100% on your game and keep moving in the midst of your overwhelmed and exhausted state, creating activity to make yourself feel productive, you run a much higher risk of making a relationship mistake and burning bridges.

When you feel overwhelmed about what to do next and feel like you could go any one of a hundred directions, give yourself permission to take a breather. It will bring peace and direction back to your mind and help you more clearly identify what to do next.

4. YOU'RE DESPERATE TO CLOSE A DEAL

Have you ever been in a conversation where the salesperson was desperate to close the deal? It became all about the salesperson instead of your needs, didn't it?

This is dangerous ground, because desperation can be sensed by your prospect before you ever start speaking, and it creates an atmosphere that repels instead of attracts.

So, before you walk into a room or pick up the phone, you need to make a conscious choice that you're going to release the outcome and let it go.

If you're releasing the outcome, then what do you care about? You care about the prospect you're meeting with, and they will know it.

You want the best for them, that's why you're there. The outcome will resolve itself. Just release it. If the prospect senses you're really working in their best interest, then your desperation won't spoil the outcome and you'll be much more likely to close a deal.

Also, don't follow up with your prospect before the day and time you've scheduled, unless you have a valid business reason for doing so.

There have been times when I would check in with a prospect just two or three days after my initial sales conversation—because I was desperate—even though we agreed to a follow-up appointment a full week later. Doing this almost always worked against me unless I had a valid business reason for making the contact before the agreed time.

Ex-Notre Dame football coach Lou Holtz has guidance for this situation. In fact, it's guidance for **any** situation in the form of an acronym: WIN. It stands for **What's Important Now?**

The answer to that question, whatever it may be, will direct your next step, if you're willing to be honest with the answer instead of letting worry, fear, or anxiety control your actions.

Your decisions control your destiny. So, ask yourself: what's important now?

5. THE PROSPECT HAS A LONG-TERM RELATIONSHIP WITH ANOTHER VENDOR

When you ask your prospect questions during the interview

process, you should always try to get a sense of the strength of the relationship they have with their current vendor, if any.

If they have a good, long-term relationship with another vendor, explain that you can respect that, because you have many great long-term relationships with your clients as well.

Then follow up by asking this, "I'm just curious: are you married to that vendor?"

Most of the time, they'll say, "Well, no." Follow that by asking, "OK, if I could show you something that you felt was a better fit, do you think we'd have a fair opportunity to earn your business, or would we just be wasting each other's time?"

I've had some prospects say, "Honestly, I think we'd just be wasting each other's time, because the vendor we use is on our board," or it's the CEO's brother or something similar. At that point, you just thank them for their honesty and graciously end the conversation.

Others have said, "If what you have to offer is better, I think you'd have a fair shot at earning our business."

The key is getting that on the table as early as possible, so it doesn't blindside you at the end of your conversation.

6. YOU HAVE NO LEADS AND NOTHING IN YOUR SALES PIPELINE

Without leads, you're dead; that is just a fact in selling. Unless you have an existing book of business and/or your company has a proven lead generation mechanism, the number one most important activity of any salesperson, besides knowing how to sell, is generating leads. If you get leads, the sales will take care of themselves, as long as you are honing those skills.

Many say that cold-call lead generation is dead. Is it the most efficient way to produce leads? Not usually. But it's definitely not dead.

The approach I personally used when starting in straight-commission sales worked beautifully to help me book appointments a week or more in advance, with people I never met, several states away.

Those I've taught this to often double and triple the number of appointments they set.

It's called **"The Assumptive Appointment Solution"** and I've included it as a bonus chapter at the end of this book.

I also have a proven lead generation tool that has provided, on average, a five-to-one return on investment. It utilizes direct mail pointing to a custom landing page based on a specific offer.

I call it **"Lead Generation Magic."** You can get a free copy of it at: TheSellingFormula.com.

The bottom line is that you need a reliable lead generation process that works for you, or sales just won't happen.

7. YOU COMPLETELY FORGOT WHAT YOU WERE SAYING DURING YOUR SALES CONVERSATION

Now, this may seem a little unnecessary to address as a "Top Selling Challenge," but it happens.

Occasionally, I've had sales calls where I've been mid-sentence and literally forgotten what I was saying. It's a horrible feeling. I would apologize and explain that I had been traveling for days or that I was short on sleep and just lost what I was saying. There's nothing wrong with admitting it.

What you don't want to do is just wing it. You might be way off point and come across as crazy. You might say something you don't mean. You might try covering it up with a load of BS. And as a salesperson, that's the last impression you want to give people.

Be honest if you've forgotten what you were saying. This establishes your truthfulness. Besides, you're not the first person it has ever happened to. Others will relate to you. This might even break the tension, as people recall funny instances of when it happened to them. It humanizes you. And that is the honest impression you want to give as a salesperson.

8. BEING USED IN THE DUE-DILIGENCE PROCESS

This one is brutal. If you have ever found out at the end of a meeting that your prospect was just doing "research" or seeing what else was out there, you know how used it can make you feel.

If you get the sense during your conversation that the other person is not really listening wholeheartedly or they're pushing you along to get your price, these are indicators that something is working against you.

Here are a couple key questions you should ask during your interview: "Are you looking at other vendors right now for this type of product/service?" and "Who is your current provider for this product/service?"

If they already have a provider, ask what their biggest frustration is right now. If they cannot articulate one, perhaps they are just using you as leverage for better pricing. Don't wait until you are through with your presentation to find out.

There's a possibility that a deal has already been signed with your competitor, and the prospect is just using you to round out their due-diligence requirement of getting three quotes from other vendors.

Another possibility is that they already have a provider and are using you as leverage for a better deal with them, with no intention of switching to your offer.

Do your best to get this information out on the table early in your interview so you know what you're up against and can adapt your sales conversation accordingly.

9. YOU AREN'T CONNECTING WITH THE PROSPECT—BAD RAPPORT

It happens. Sometimes, no matter how well you try to match and mirror a prospect, or how empathetic you are, their body language and tone of voice indicate they're closed off to you and would really prefer you just leave their office.

It may be true, or it may not be true.

So, instead of plowing ahead and hoping this turns out well, pause and say, "May I ask you a question? I get the sense that perhaps this isn't a good time for us to have a conversation. Is everything OK?"

Sometimes the prospect will get offended that you asked, because they really just have a sour demeanor and that's who they are—bless their heart.

You can then say, "Alright, I was just curious if everything was OK," and continue the discussion.

However, most of the time, I see a physical reaction from that question, like the prospect was daydreaming and is suddenly jolted back into reality. They were, in fact, pre-occupied and had something else on their mind.

Ask them if this is a good time to have a discussion or if you should reschedule. I've had prospects admit they just got out of a difficult meeting or had to deal with an emergency, but, out of respect for my time, kept the meeting.

Unless it's you—and it could be, so be careful—bad rapport may be a result of your prospect having something else on their mind. That's why, in the connection step of the conversation, I found it's important to ask if they've had to put out any fires today. It will work to your advantage to help regain your prospect's attention if you can get this out in the open before your sales conversation ever starts.

10. JUST TELL ME, HOW MUCH IS IT?

If you are interrupted during your sales conversation by the question—"Just tell me, how much is it?"—answer with the question: "I'm curious, is price your only concern?"

Most prospects will say it's not their only concern, but it's important. Fair enough.

Respond by saying: "Great question. I'm not sure you qualify for what we're offering. That's why I'm asking you these questions. Also, I've found that if I don't provide some context for the pricing and all that's included with our product/service, it won't make a lot of sense. So, are you OK with continuing our conversation, or did you want me to stop here?"

Most prospects will let you continue as long as they know where you're going in the conversation. So, provide a quick preview with, "OK here's what we'll discuss next...then we'll get to pricing."

If they say "No, just give me the bottom line, I don't have all day," then give them a range of pricing from high to low. "It's typically $299 to $79 a month, depending upon the options you choose."

Then they'll probably ask, "What are the options?" and you can say, "That's exactly where I was going. Did you want me to explain the options, or should we stop here?"

11. YOUR PRICE IS TOO HIGH

If your prospect says, "Your price is too high," understand that this is usually a knee-jerk negotiating tactic called "flinching" that's designed to get you to have a knee-jerk response of somehow lowering your price.

Because this is a relative issue, simply respond by saying, "Compared to what?"

Compared to similar products or services, your price may be just fine; compared to doing nothing, maybe it's high; and compared to its actual value, it might be considered rather low. So, compared to what?

If the prospect responds by saying, "Compared to your competition," then ask if price is their only concern, or are they concerned about...and start listing off key benefits you can stack on top of one another. For example:

"Is price your only concern, or are you concerned about service, compatibility, quality, and the experiences of other clients...?" Or any other key benefits you can stack on top of one another to help the prospect see that there are other important factors to consider besides price.

Recall, as well, that you should offer three different price points if possible. That flexibility is designed to minimize the high price question, because you in fact have a lower-priced option as well.

Another way to address the issue is by asking how far apart you and your prospect are on price. If you get a direct answer, it's yet another opportunity to earn their business.

Maybe you can't get down to that price—and ideally you really don't want to, otherwise you're making it all about price, and that's a losing proposition—but you might be able to offset that differential with some other incentive or guarantee.

Bear in mind that price is always a function of perceived value. Somebody may think $1 million is too high. Somebody else might think it's a bargain. It just depends on the value they place on your offer. The more perceived value your offer can show, the lower the probability your prospect will be focused on price.

12. YOUR PROSPECT WANTS TO "THINK ABOUT IT"

If you're prospect says they want to "think about it," ask them, "Help me understand: what is it that you need to think about?"

Is there something you have not explained well enough? Is there something you should clarify? Is there some objection that hasn't been addressed?

If you can get what it is they need to think about on the table, say, "That's a great question." Then provide the answer. Then immediately follow that up with, "Is there anything else you're thinking about?" Keep doing that until you've addressed each question.

Then go back to closing the deal with, "OK, is there any reason we couldn't move forward today?" This is stated in the negative, so that answering no actually means yes.

Finally, it may well be the case that this person does not have the power to authorize a deal. If the person you're talking with is not the decision-maker, you need to find out who is and how to proceed. Ask the question: "Is there someone else who needs to be involved in this decision that you'd like me to connect with?"

The bottom line is that you should never leave a sales conversation with someone who wants to "think about it" without asking what they need to think about and attempting to flush out an answer.

Again, your goal is to get a yes or no. A "think about it" might as well be a no. If they're not persuaded to move forward now, "thinking about it" is typically a way to get you out the door, because they just don't want to tell you no, and they don't want to talk about your offer any more.

13. IT'S NOT IN THE BUDGET

The "it's not in the budget" objection is given for several reasons, most of which are typically not related to the budget at all.

First, it's a great way for a prospect who's not interested in your offer to shut you down and tell you no without it looking like they're actually telling you no.

What a great way for a prospect to get you out of their

office, right? I mean, if they don't have the means to purchase your offering, what do you do?

Well, you leave.

And if they aren't persuaded that the value of your offer is worthy of realigning their budget dollars to purchase from you, that's what will happen.

That's why, during your interview, you should ask a question about budget. For example, "Is this something that, if you wanted it, you'd have the budget flexibility to move forward with?" They may say yes, or that they don't know, because it depends upon what they see. That's OK. At least you put the question out there.

But the fact is, if someone wants something badly enough, they will figure out a way to buy it.

So, if you've done your best to show the value of your offer, and they still say, "It's not in the budget," then ask this question: "Let's say I could provide this to you for free, would you be interested in giving it a try?" If they say no, then it's obviously over.

However, if they say yes, then find out what it would take

to move the deal forward, because the door is still open—as long as they're not being unreasonable.

Another reason for this response may be that the person you're speaking with doesn't have the authority to purchase from you. It happens. You simply weren't talking with the right person. You always want to find that out.

During your interview, be sure to ask whether there is someone else aside from your prospect who might need to be involved in the decision-making process.

Another consideration is that, although they may not think they have the budget to purchase, it's up to you to help them find the budget dollars.

For example, with prospects that do billboard advertising, I would point out that the cost of that type of advertising would easily pay for the investment in our service, which will provide a significantly better return on investment. You're just getting them to see how realigning their budget with your offer may prove to be a superior use of their dollars.

Finally, the budget might legitimately be tied up, and there really aren't available funds to purchase your offer, yet there's strong interest. This can often happen in the final quarter of your prospect's fiscal year.

When that's the case, perhaps you can offer to split an invoice between the current fiscal year and the next to make it financially feasible. Or, sign a deal now, pending implementation in the next fiscal year.

Finally, your prospect might be in a multiyear deal with another vendor. In which case, simply find out when you need to circle back with them and put that information into your follow-up notes. Then follow up when it's time.

Some will close, some will not. Just keep putting things into your sales funnel.

14. THIS REQUIRES BOARD APPROVAL

Assuming your offer needs board approval, and it's been added to the agenda for discussion, there are three things you want to do, in descending order. First, you want to find out if a vendor such as yourself would be allowed to make a presentation at the board meeting.

If you can, that's great, but if not, the next best thing is to see if you can get an introduction to any of the board members to present your offer. Find out who the more outspoken and passionate members of the board—who tend to carry the decisions—are, in order to "soften the ground" for your solution and get buy-in ahead of the meeting.

This is critical, because there are typically many agenda items, and your offer may only be given five minutes for discussion. If your offer has some vocal supporters, your chance of gaining approval will be greatly improved.

Finally, find out what information the board needs in order to approve your offer. Then provide an executive summary of your offer—along with a special incentive and deadline—that will be included in the board packet of information given to each member that explains the meeting's agenda items. Otherwise, the discussion on your offer may literally be just one minute long and consist of these questions: what is it, how does it work, and how much does it cost?

The additional details from the executive summary, along with at least one champion on the board, can help move your offer forward to approval. With no champion on the board or supporting documentation with an incentive to move forward now, your offer will likely be dead on arrival.

15. YOU WANT TO QUIT SELLING

Selling isn't for the faint of heart. Sometimes you just have to grind it out and persevere day after day. Doing the right things and being consistent will bring victory.

But what if it doesn't?

What if you're doing the right things, grinding it out day after day, and it's not working? There are many reasons it may not be working, and the reality is that most of those can be addressed with proper coaching or mentoring.

However, what cannot be fixed is a mismatch between your gifts and what you do on a daily basis to earn a living. If you believe selling is just not for you, then I strongly recommend you find whatever it is that makes you come alive and do that instead.

But how?

You need to know your personal strengths and align yourself with them. It's far better to develop your strengths than to work on your weaknesses.

Now, we all need to address our weaknesses. Most of us are painfully aware of them. But that's not what I'm talking about here. I'm talking about developing your

God-given strengths to become the best version of yourself vocationally.

One of the most powerful tools I've found to help identify those strengths is a book, which comes with an online test, titled *StrengthsFinder 2.0* by Tom Rath. It will pinpoint your strengths with amazing accuracy. If you feel mismatched with your vocation, or are just looking for a way to affirm your strengths, you need to take this test.

There was a gentleman I hired and worked with for several months who just wouldn't follow the proven process we had for selling our service. So finally, I had to give him a 30-day ultimatum.

He had to hit a specific sales quota in 30 days, or he was going to have to move on to another job. He barely met the 30-day quota and was totally burned out after hitting it. In fact, he was devastated when he understood that he was going to have to hit that mark again the next month, and the next month, and the month after that.

I told him to go do something he loved. You know what? He landed in a completely different industry and is doing very well. The fact is, if you don't love this business, and it doesn't energize you, you're probably not going to succeed in it. It may be time for you to look at something else.

CHAPTER 10

BECOMING A SELLING MASTER

Most of us live two lives. The life we live, and the unlived life within us. Between the two stands Resistance.

—STEVEN PRESSFIELD

In the beginning of this book, I mentioned that you were destined for greater things. What will keep you from achieving greater things is resistance.

In his book *The War of Art*, Steven Pressfield magnificently details all the many ways that resistance works to prevent us from making the difference we were created to make in this world.

Once we have an awareness of all the subtle ways resistance manifests, from our own mental self-sabotage, hidden addictions, and worthless habits, to the drama of life around us, we recognize that we're in a battle.

We're in a battle that has massive consequences for our lives. If you think I'm overstating this, then look at the lives of those you're closest to. What forces do you see that are keeping your loved ones from fulfilling their purpose?

What forces are keeping you from fulfilling your purpose?

YOUR HABITS

Most of how we think and what we do is driven, for better or worse, by our habits.

Change your habits, change your life. It's that simple and that profound.

Take a look at your day. Are the habit patterns you've established supporting your efforts to become what you were created to become, or are they sabotaging them?

If your habits aren't helping you, what new habit do you need to implement? What do you need to start or stop doing today that will help you become the person you know you can become?

You could literally be one habit away from a massive shift in your life. What's the one thing that you could start doing today that, if you kept doing it daily, would have the most profound impact on your life and the lives of those around you?

What does this have to do with selling? Everything.

As you improve yourself, you improve your selling. Self-improvement and improved selling are linked together like water and rain. You can't have one without the other.

We tend to go on autopilot when something is working "well enough." Unless we absolutely hit rock bottom, we usually don't take action to change something. So, we just keep doing what we've always done.

How many years have you been in sales? Have you had 10 years of experience, or one year of experience repeated 10 times?

Are you continuing to do the same things expecting different results?

You've probably heard the saying that big doors turn on small hinges. You've also probably heard the Pareto principle: "20% of the invested input is responsible for 80% of the results obtained."

Ultimately, only a few things really impact our success.

That's why I don't recommend wholesale changes to everything you're doing all at once. If you did that, then there would be no way to know which change really made the critical difference for you. Therefore, focus on one piece of your selling process at a time.

Right now, what's the one thing you could focus on that would have the greatest impact on your selling efforts, the highest leverage? Then work on that now. Become great at that one thing. Then move to the next, while keeping an eye out for other ways to get better at what you just improved.

Think about it in terms of a golf swing. If you're a golfer and are struggling with some aspect of your game, chances are you have a tiny glitch somewhere between your address and your follow-through.

Maybe your grip is wrong, maybe your balance is off, or maybe you are turning your wrists over too soon. But what you want to do is examine each step in the swing and tweak it, rather than adopt a brand-new swing all at once.

A new swing would be entirely foreign to you, and if something is wrong with any of its components, you won't have any idea where to begin to fix it.

Most of us understand internally, in our gut, where we're struggling. If not, that's where a sales manager, partner, or mentor can be very helpful. Have that person go on a ride-along to observe you or listen to a recording of your sales calls to help you discover your strengths and weaknesses.

To return to the metaphor: it's like having a swing coach who can video you, then show you what's going wrong and how to fix it.

We get stuck inside our own bottle and need help reading the writing on our label. Record yourself on a live sales discussion, and then listen to the recording. It will be a dramatic eye-opener, because it allows you to hear what you're saying from a third-party perspective and critique it "outside your bottle."

Maybe you're saying to yourself, "That all sounds good, but I need results right now!" Well, that's how you get there: one single high-leverage improvement followed by another.

The reality is that you may only need one tweak to your

sales process to dramatically impact your results right now. It could be just one question you're not asking that, if you started asking it, could shift everything for you.

COMMITMENT TO CONTINUOUS LEARNING

Every great salesperson I know is a continuous learner. They feed themselves constantly with information and inspiration that can give them a nuanced way of saying something better, asking one powerful question they've never thought of asking, or asking it differently.

Experiment and test. If you have trouble closing, spend the next week testing a different closing question or questions. But keep in mind that every step in your sales process builds on the previous one.

For example, if you haven't set a clear agenda at the beginning of your sales conversation, haven't asked great questions during the interview, and failed to connect the value of your offer to your prospect's needs, trying different closing questions isn't going to help much.

So, you need to pull back and look at your sales process. Look at each step using The Selling Formula as a guide and rank your performance on a scale of one to 10, with 10 being the best.

How are you doing with:

1. Connecting
2. Interview questions
3. Presenting your solution
4. Pricing and guarantees
5. Closing

Look at where you've ranked yourself lowest, focus on that, and improve it. Then move on to the next thing.

RELIEF VS. RESULTS

When I experienced prolonged periods of time without closing a deal, I would stress out like a drug addict who needed a fix. Then I'd close a deal and be on a high for a little while afterward, but then start feeling uptight again, saying to myself, "Man, I have got to close another deal!"

Yes, there is something euphoric about getting deals done. But to live in constant cycles of feast and famine can bring overwhelming stress into our lives and absolutely wear us out physically and emotionally, so that we have nothing left to give to the people who are closest to us.

I call this the freak-out and relief cycle.

You can identify it by completing this statement: "If I could just get [fill in the blank], everything would be all right." The problem is that if you get that thing exactly, it will still only provide temporary relief. It won't give you permanent change. Inevitably, the same situation will return.

Relief is temporary; consistent results require a change in our way of life. They require new habits.

Rather than living in the constant cycle of freak-out and relief, proactively and methodically improving your sales process will move you to a more predictable sales experience and income stream. Isn't that what you want?

I often sponsor a golf hole at various annual tournaments around the country and see many of the same people year after year. I'll never forget one woman in particular. Every year she had a different set of clubs, or a new driver, or different shoes, or a new putter, but her game never improved.

When I asked how her golf game was going, she said, "No matter how hard I try, I just can't seem to buy my game!"

Instead of investing in her game through coaching and consistent focus, she would buy the newest club or latest fashion.

Instead of making a permanent change in our habits, we get distracted from the hard work of self-improvement by purchasing the latest shiny object that grabs our attention. You can't buy your sales game. There's no substitute for focused, methodical improvement. It takes work.

Maybe it's some new app for our phone, or an online scheduling calendar, or an upgraded version of some customer relationship software. Now, to be sure, those can be great tools to help our productivity. However, if we're really honest, they aren't helping with the real need: improving our personal selling process.

Perhaps you're addicted to education, and this book is another of many that will sit on your shelf with others that have great advice, but from which you'll apply nothing. If that makes you feel angry, good. I hope you'll do something about it. Of course, I am saying this with love— really, I am.

I've been lifting weights for years, and it's been a lesson in slow but steady development. If you have ever spent hours in the gym to see only microscopic progress, you understand how advertisers get rich selling get-fit-quick products.

There are ads on all the time trying to convince you that,

if you buy this or that piece of equipment, or this or that set of videos, you, too, will lose 30 pounds and have abs of steel in just six weeks.

The problem is that you can't buy a magazine-cover body with your credit card while watching late-night TV. Fitness isn't something that comes in a package; it's a lifestyle that requires continuous upkeep and focus.

That piece of gym equipment or video series you purchase might give you a sense of having actually done something, because you pressed the "buy" button or called up and gave your credit card information. But chances are it's just going to end up collecting dust somewhere before it's eventually sold for pennies on the dollar in a garage sale or thrown away.

The same holds true for any worthwhile endeavor, especially sales. Great results come through effort focused on improving your highest-leverage activities.

Here are some key things you can do to immediately move yourself toward becoming a selling master.

KEEP A JOURNAL

Keep a sales journal to track your progress. It's amazing

what putting your thoughts down in writing after a sales discussion can do for you.

It's a powerful way to debrief and pinpoint where you think you did well and where you could have improved. It's another way to help you get outside your bottle and see what you're doing from a different perspective, so you can consider how to do it better.

Keeping a sales journal is also a great accountability tool and gauge of your progress. The simple act of going back and reading your notes will trigger your mind to consider different ways and means of improving your selling process.

THE NUMBER ONE SHORTCUT TO SELLING SUCCESS

Here is the fastest way to double your sales effectiveness:

Audio-record your top salesperson's presentation and listen to it at least 25 times. Really listen to it. Memorize it. Own the exact language and script they follow and duplicate it. That's your shortcut to success.

In the major corporations I've worked for, including Coca-Cola and Johnson & Johnson, I never once recall the company taking the top two or three salespeople, recording their live selling conversations, and then sending them out to the field sales team, saying, "Say what these people say, in the order they say it, exactly as they say it."

I don't understand why companies don't do this. They will spend countless dollars and hours on sales training when they could shortcut the entire process by doing this one simple thing. Identify the best reps, see which one has the most consistent process, and have the other members of the sales team copy it. You now have a distinct process with which you can judge the progress of your sales team.

One caveat here: of course, everyone has their own individual selling style. I'm not suggesting that you ignore your unique personality for the sake of exact duplication. However, I am suggesting that, like a great actor, you memorize and use the same lines as your top performer if you want to experience similar success.

GET GROUP OR ONE-ON-ONE COACHING

Group or one-on-one coaching is definitely worth checking out. Some of the best advice I've gotten has been from talking to another person who has overcome the same problem I've experienced. There's nothing more rewarding than taking a piece of advice, applying it on your next sales call, and seeing immediate results.

READ BOOKS AND LISTEN TO PODCASTS

Immerse yourself in books, podcasts, and online training. If you spend hours in your car, you can obtain an MBA-level education—probably better than an MBA—by choosing to use that time to feed yourself with great selling instruction and encouragement.

Zig Ziglar used to call his vehicle "a university on wheels."

Some of the greatest sales and marketing ideas I've heard have come by using drive time to learn something new.

WHAT NOW

There's always a reason why something "isn't working." You can figure it out by being brutally honest with yourself. It's not magic; it's about identifying the problem, taking 100% ownership of it, and then choosing to do what it takes to overcome it. That really is the key to life.

I have included more information on my website, TheSellingFormula.com. There, you will also be able to get a copy of "Lead Generation Magic," which has provided a minimum five-to-one return on investment every time I've implemented it.

TWO VOICES

I leave you with this very personal piece of advice.

Inevitably there will be times when you're feeling completely overwhelmed and exhausted. Your head may feel like it's about to explode, and your gut is tied in knots. You can't seem to pull the right lever to make anything work. In fact, you can't even think straight or prioritize your next step, because all the options seem hidden.

To top it off, there's this voice whispering to you that you're going to fail, everything's going to fall apart, and you won't succeed. Ever been there?

What do you do?

You stop. Stop what you're doing. Walk away for a while. Take a break. Give yourself permission to pause for 20 or 30 minutes and rest. Close your eyes. Breathe deeply. Seriously, take a nap.

When overwhelmed, I've been amazed how purposely

unplugging from a situation can dramatically improve my outlook and help me see the next step forward.

I've discovered there are two voices speaking to us: the one that encourages us and the one we hear when we're run down and exhausted.

One is telling you how great you can be. I think it is the truth about who you were created to be and the gifts and calling inside of you. This comes from your spirit.

The other voice, the one that tries to sabotage you, arises from your flesh. It speaks negative, self-defeating words.

What you feed grows, and what you starve dies.

What will you choose to feed in your life? Your spirit or your flesh?

Choose wisely, because you were destined for greater things.

I wish you the very best and hope to hear about your successes in applying The Selling Formula. My email address is, Brian@TheSellingFormula.com.

TOP 10 MOST POWERFUL SELLING PHRASES YOU SHOULD BE USING RIGHT NOW

The phrases you're about to read are absolutely some of the most powerful and reliable you can use in any selling situation to close, trial close, ask for clarification, or request a next step.

These top 10 power phrases are the result of thousands of prospect and customer interactions.

They have helped triple my income and are proven to

enhance trust and rapport when used with sincerity and integrity.

THE MASTER KEY TO SELLING SUCCESS

I can tell you unequivocally that the master key to selling success is encapsulated in one simple truth:

THE QUESTIONS YOU ASK WILL DIRECTLY DETERMINE THE RESULTS YOU ACHIEVE.

Ask the same questions: get the same results.

Ask different questions: get different results.

Here's an example: imagine that you're cold-calling a business. You walk in the door and encounter the receptionist—also lovingly known as the gatekeeper.

They're called *gatekeepers* for a reason.

You can have the best product or service in the universe when you walk in that door, but if you ask the receptionist the question, "May I speak with your business manager?" do you know what you're going to hear?

Sure you do.

- Who are you?
- Do you have an appointment?
- What are you selling?
- Do you have a business card?
- Do you have some literature you can leave with me?

Then you're told, "If you can leave some literature and a business card, I'll be happy to pass your information along to our business manager and he will call you if he's interested."

Wow, that should make you feel like you just hit a home run. After that, you know you're going to get a call back and get invited in to make a sale, don't you?

Who are you kidding?

You're the umpteenth person who has come in that day or called asking the same question.

You've heard the definition of insanity: doing the same thing over and over and expecting different results. So why don't you ask a different question?

For example, if you're selling a particular service that reduces a physician's practice risk, you could ask, "Who in this office is responsible for mitigating risk in your practice?"

If you're selling a marketing service for the phone system, you could ask, "If I called your office and got put on hold right now, what would I hear?"

As you can see, this is much different than asking to speak with a business manager, office manager, or some other person in charge.

The point is that if you engage the gatekeeper with a question they aren't used to hearing, this interrupts their habitual response. It opens up the possibility for dialogue that could move you further down the sales path than virtually anyone else who has walked in the door or called on the phone that day, week, or even month.

In the same way, if you ask your prospects disarming questions they aren't used to hearing, you immediately open up possibilities in your sales conversations that could dramatically increase your odds of earning their business.

Your questions matter. I cannot emphasize this enough.

WHAT'S SPECIAL ABOUT THESE TOP 10 POWER PHRASES?

They grant you permission to ask your next question.

They are softeners for your questions.

They are like servants who humbly deliver your questions.

The benefit is that they enhance the bond of trust between you and your prospect. And trust is the currency for all great sales transactions.

All these phrases can stand alone and should be used that way. However, there's *extra power* when you combine them. I'll give you examples throughout this chapter.

Though some may seem obvious, *I can assure you* that they work when applied to your carefully crafted questions and personal conversations. So please do not dismiss any of these with a "well—whatever, I've heard that" response.

Let's dive in.

POWER PHRASE #1: "I'M JUST CURIOUS…"

I'm just curious: would you like to know one of the most disarming and perfectly natural phrases you can use in any selling situation? I thought you would. The beauty of this phrase is that you can use it to preface virtually ANY question.

I'm just curious: if there was anything you'd like to see changed in your current situation, what would it be?

I'm just curious: has anyone ever offered to explain the benefits of a reverse mortgage to you?

I'm just curious: when would you like to have a quick phone call?

I'm just curious: in your opinion, what would be the best outcome for our meeting today?

I'm just curious: was there a specific reason you wanted to meet with me today?

POWER PHRASE #2: "WOULD YOU BE OPPOSED TO...?"

This is perhaps one of the most extraordinary power phrases, because to answer affirmatively, the respondent must say no, which is most people's natural tendency. When you combine it with Power Phrase #1, the results are almost magical.

Would you be opposed to connecting with me next Tuesday for a quick 10-minute meeting?

Would you be opposed to seeing how our concierge services have dramatically helped other clients?

Would you be opposed to getting together by phone tomorrow morning at 9:30 a.m.?

Would you be opposed to finding out why we have a 90% renewal rate with our clients?

Would you be opposed to putting me on the agenda at your next board meeting?

To make these phrases even better, just add the words from Power Phrase #1—"I'm just curious"—to the beginning of the question.

For example:

I'm just curious: would you be opposed to connecting with me next Tuesday for a quick 10-minute meeting?

I'm just curious: would you be opposed to inviting your president into our meeting tomorrow?

I'm just curious: would you be opposed to giving me your honest opinion about our work?

POWER PHRASE #3: "IF I COULD, WOULD YOU...?"

If I could give you a phrase that would be perfect for getting a feel for someone's interest level in a particular offer, would you like to know what it is? It's Power Phrase #3.

If I could offer you some incentive to move forward now, as opposed to later, **would you** like to see it?

If I could increase your revenue 20% by changing just one phrase you use in your daily sales conversations, **would you** be interested in trying it for yourself?

If I could guarantee you would never have to pay for another oil change again, **would you** like to know more about it?

If I could give you some feedback from other clients who were in your exact situation, **would you** like to hear it?

If I could reduce the time it takes you to prepare for an audit by 50%, **would you** like to find out how?

All you have to do is add the words "be opposed" to any of the above examples to make it still more powerful. Here are Power Phrases #3 and #2 combined:

If I could give you some feedback from other clients who were in your exact situation, **would you be opposed to** hearing it?

If I could guarantee you would never have to pay for another oil change again, **would you be opposed to** finding out more about it?

I'm just curious: if I could show you a way to triple your income within 12 months, **would you be opposed to** learning more about it?

POWER PHRASE #4: "WITH YOUR PERMISSION..."

With your permission, I'd like to give you a phrase that will virtually guarantee a positive response. These three little words are absolutely amazing in their effectiveness, because they show that you respect your prospect's wishes, while at the same time emphasizing your desire to serve them. It also takes an assumptive approach to the answer, which is important in moving sales conversations forward.

With your permission, I'll make a note to check back with you in one week. Would Monday or Tuesday be better?

With your permission, I'll go ahead and have you OK the sample agreement, pending CEO approval by Friday. Is that fair enough?

With your permission, I'll pencil in 10:00 a.m. on Tuesday to stop by and show you our new program. Is there anyone else you'd like to invite to our meeting?

With your permission, I'll let your president know you suggested I set up a brief conversation to review what we spoke about today.

With your permission, I'll have my chief technology officer reach out to your head of IT to review system compatibility and give him an opportunity to answer any questions he may have.

POWER PHRASE #5: "MAY I ASK YOU A QUESTION?"

May I ask you a question? How would you like to get more information from your prospects about their attitude regarding virtually any aspect of your offering? Then use this Power Phrase. It positions you in a consultative role and can work well at the back end of a sentence or all by itself.

Since we're speaking about that, **may I ask you a question?**

That's a good point. **May I ask you a question?**

I've been giving some thought to what you told me the other day. **May I ask you a question?**

I understand how frustrating that must be. **May I ask you a question?**

May I ask you a question?

Another way to use this is along with Power Phrase #1.

I'm just curious: may I ask you a question?

POWER PHRASE #6: "IS THERE ANY REASON WHY...?"

Is there any reason why you wouldn't like to know how your prospect feels about your offer or a specific point made in your sales conversation? This phrase is best used in conjunction with the words *couldn't*, *wouldn't*, or *shouldn't*.

The psychology of this power phrase is that, like #2—"would you be opposed to"—to answer affirmatively, the respondent must say no.

Of course, if the answer is yes, then you have a golden opportunity to find out what the objection might be and work from there.

Is there any reason why we couldn't move forward with this now?

If it were up to you, **is there any reason why** you wouldn't want to give our service a try?

Is there any reason why we shouldn't go ahead and set up the delivery date?

Is there any reason why you wouldn't want to have this installed by next week?

Is there any reason why we couldn't set up a time with your CEO to review what we've just discussed?

To add additional softening to the question, you can easily add Power Phrase #1—"I'm just curious"—to the front end of any of these questions.

For example:

I'm just curious: is there any reason why you wouldn't want to have this installed by next week?

I'm just curious: is there any reason why we shouldn't go ahead and set up the delivery date?

I'm just curious: if I could provide you with free delivery, **is there any reason why** you wouldn't want to move forward with this now?

You can also add Power Phrase #5 on the front end:

May I ask you a question? Is there any reason why you wouldn't want to implement a portion of this solution as a test?

POWER PHRASE #7: "HELP ME UNDERSTAND..."

Help me understand: would you like a great way to ask your prospect a question? This phrase is best positioned as an opener to your question and works very well when combined with other power phrases.

Although it's similar to Power Phrase #1—"I'm just curious"—it carries a deeper sense of humility, which can be very appealing to your prospect.

Help me understand: is price your only concern?

Help me understand: were there any additional questions, or do you need more information?

Help me understand: exactly what information would

you need to give to your board in order for us to move forward?

Help me understand: do you have all that you need, or did I miss something?

Help me understand: did you want this in the regular or deluxe model?

Here are some examples of using this in combination with other power phrases:

Help me understand: if I could provide you with a way to move forward now, as opposed to later, **would you** like to hear about it?

Help me understand: would you be opposed to personally introducing me to your CFO, so we could move forward with this idea?

Help me understand: is there any reason why we couldn't start this next week?

POWER PHRASE #8: "WOULDN'T YOU AGREE...?"

Wouldn't you agree that being able to ask trial closing questions during a sales discussion is a great way to determine whether you're on track with your prospect? Then this is a great phrase to use.

Wouldn't you agree there seems to be no end in sight to the increase in long-term medical care costs?

You've worked long and hard to save for your retirement, and it would be a tragedy to lose it all in taxes. **Wouldn't you agree?**

Wouldn't you agree that your productivity would explode if you could minimize all your daily distractions?

Based upon what we've discussed so far, **wouldn't you agree** that this is the easiest marketing tool you've ever seen?

This is a pretty amazing feature. **Wouldn't you agree?**

Combining this with Power Phrases #5, #7, or #1:

May I ask you a question? Wouldn't you agree that the fastest way to discover whether this is a good fit would be to just try it?

Help me understand: wouldn't you agree that, besides price, there are other significant factors to consider with this type of service?

I'm just curious: wouldn't you agree that this is the easiest-to-use marketing tool you've ever seen?

POWER PHRASE #9: "DOESN'T IT +/- MAKE SENSE?"

Doesn't it make sense to confirm critical details during your sales discussion? You can combine these words or use them independently. The bottom line is that they work.

Doesn't it make sense to lock your tuition costs in now with a guarantee they won't rise when your children start college?

Doesn't it make you wonder why other companies focus on price when, as we've just discussed, there are so many other important factors to consider?

When you consider all the options, this one seems to **make** the most **sense, doesn't it?**

So, **doesn't it make sense** to consider this a revenue generator instead of an expense?

Having a proprietary feature like this **makes sense, doesn't it?**

I'm just curious: doesn't it make sense to give this a try?

POWER PHRASE #10: "WOULD +/- WOULDN'T IT?"

By definition, the word "would" is a verb and indicates action on something that's *going to happen*. The power of this phrase is that it can be positioned into your question to get agreement from your prospect about actually using your product or service.

If having a system that virtually eliminates monthly maintenance is something you're looking for, then it **would** be good timing to move forward with this, **wouldn't it?**

You'd probably agree that our competitor's product is designed for IT experts, which **would** make it difficult for non IT people to use, **wouldn't it?**

Based upon what you've seen so far, **wouldn't it** make sense to give this a try?

Since you'd like to budget this for next year, if we could get you started now for just a one-time installation fee, that **would** be fair, **wouldn't it?**

All things being equal, you'd probably agree that choosing our Platinum Option **would** be the best solution for you, **wouldn't it?**

I'm just curious: if we could add a 90-day money-back guarantee, it would be worth trying, **wouldn't it**?

NEXT STEPS

The best way to apply these is to first build your interview questions as outlined in Chapter 5, then integrate power phrases into them, and then test your responses.

A great starting point is to use Power Phrase #3, "If I could, would you..." in your closing conversation. For example: "**If I could** provide you with some incentive to move forward now, rather than later, **would you** be opposed to hearing about it?"

Try one power phrase, master it, and then add others.

As mentioned, the questions you ask will directly determine the results you achieve.

Ask the same questions: get the same results.

Ask different questions: get different results.

I'm curious; wouldn't it be worth it to ask different questions?

THE ASSUMPTIVE APPOINTMENT SOLUTION™

If you learn the techniques I'm about to show you here, you'll greatly reduce the amount of rejection that comes with cold-calling, and the hit-or-miss, time-sucking uncertainty so common with that approach.

Instead, you'll be able to set appointments by phone and build your travel schedule around key appointments you've confirmed, as opposed to physically cold-calling and hoping that someone decides to meet with you.

What you'll get is a more consistent, predictable means of

appointment-setting that gives you better control of your schedule, instead of being held hostage by your prospects' random schedules.

At the heart of this approach is "assuming" your prospect will meet with you unless you're told otherwise. The general rule here is that it's better to assume the appointment than to approach a prospect with a request for a meeting. You'll see exactly what I mean in a moment.

Here are the steps:

1. Choose your target prospects in a specific area that you plan to go to about eight to 10 days in advance.
2. Call your target prospects and leave a voicemail for them—sample scripts below—indicating you'll be in their area on a specific day and time and that, with their permission, you'll stop by for no more than five to 10 minutes to introduce them to your offering.
3. If you don't hear anything from them, leave a follow-up voicemail two to three days ahead of your assumed appointment, confirming the day and time of your meeting.
4. Show up at the appointed time.

So, instead of walking into your prospect's place of business cold and requesting a meeting, you call and tell them you're going to be in their area on a specific day and time, and ask if they'd be opposed to meeting with you for no more than five to 10 minutes while you're in the area.

This approach works whether you're in the same city or several states away. I know, because it's exactly what I did to start and grow my business.

What you want to do is get at least one prospect to confirm an appointment with you. That becomes your "anchor" appointment. From there, you reach out to other prospects within a certain radius in the same geographic area and set additional appointments.

Here's how it works:

You start with Voicemail Script #1 below. Then, after you have your anchor appointment, you switch to Voicemail Script #2, referencing the confirmed appointment to create curiosity in your prospect's mind: "Hmm, if he's meeting with someone else nearby, maybe I should meet with him too."

Here's Voicemail Script #1 with fictitious information filled in. You'll find the actual script at the end of the chapter.

VOICEMAIL SCRIPT #1

Bob, have a quick question for you. This is Brian Robinson with The Selling Formula. My number is 555-455-4455 and I'm going to be in Elmhurst next Tuesday, May 5th, around 10:00 in the morning and wondered if you would be opposed to me stopping by for no more than five to 10 minutes.

We work with hundreds of other businesses like yours, providing a five-step formula that can double your sales within 90 days. So, with your permission, I was going to go ahead and pencil in next Tuesday to stop by.

Of course, I don't know your schedule, so if that doesn't work, if you could kindly let me know, I would appreciate it. Otherwise, I look forward to seeing you next Tuesday the 5th at 10:00 a.m. Thanks, Bob. Again, my number is 555-455-4455.

Now, you can also leave your email address after your phone number, but I caution you that it makes it too easy for your prospect to email you back and tell you not to show up. Really, you WANT them to call you back.

Now, sometimes you'll catch your contact live instead of leaving a voicemail. In that case, you adjust your appointment-setting script and say the following:

LIVE SCRIPT #1

Hi Bob, quick question. This is Brian Robinson. I'm going to be in Elmhurst next Tuesday the 5th around 10:00 a.m. and wondered if you would be opposed to me stopping by for no more than five to 10 minutes to introduce you to what we're doing with [many, hundreds, etc.] other businesses in the area.

Then pause and wait for a response.

In a live phone call, I purposely do not tell the prospect the company name, but act as if they should know me.

They immediately begin scanning their mental contact list thinking, "Brian Robinson...Brian Robinson...do I know this guy? He's going to be in town next week and wants to meet...Should I know this guy? He only wants five to 10 minutes...what does his company do?"

Then your prospect will say, "What do you do?" or "Who are you with?" or "What's your name again?" You simply answer their question and continue with the script:

> We provide a five-step formula that's helped our clients double their sales within 90 days, and I was just wondering if you'd be opposed to me stopping by for no more than five to 10 minutes, just to ask you a few quick questions and show you what we're doing with other businesses in your area.

What's important here is your benefit statement. Unless your company is well-known in your space, you want to lead with the benefit you provide, as opposed to your company name. The prospect will ask for your company name and other details when you book the appointment if they're sufficiently interested.

Now, once you've booked your anchor appointment, you can adjust the script to reference that appointment in order to create credibility and curiosity because someone else has agreed to meet with you. I've underlined the change in the script below.

VOICEMAIL SCRIPT #2

Bob, this is Brian Robinson with The Selling Formula. My number is 555-455-4455, and I'm going to be in town next Tuesday, May 5th, meeting with Jim Smith over at Deluxe Brands; and while I'm in the area, wondered if you'd be opposed to me stopping by around 11:00 a.m. for no more than five to 10 minutes to introduce you to what we're doing with hundreds of other businesses like yours.

We offer a five-step formula that helps our clients double their sales within 90 days. So, with your permission, I was going to pencil in next Tuesday to stop by.

Of course, I don't know your schedule, so if that doesn't work, if you could kindly let me know, I would appreciate it. Otherwise I look forward to seeing you next Tuesday the 5th at 11:00 a.m. Thanks, Bob. Again, my number is 555-455-4455.

Now, if you catch your contact live, you adjust your script accordingly.

LIVE SCRIPT #2

Hi Bob, quick question; this is Brian Robinson <u>and I'm going to be in town next Tuesday, May 5th, meeting with Jim Smith over at Deluxe Brands</u>; and while I'm in the area, wondered if you'd be opposed to me stopping by around 11:00 a.m. for no more than five to 10 minutes to introduce you to what we're doing.

Pause and wait for a response from the prospect.

Again, your prospect will likely ask one of three questions: "What do you do?" or "Who are you with?" or "What's your name again?" You simply answer their question and continue with the script:

We provide a five-step formula that's helped our clients double their sales in about 90 days, and I was wondering if you'd be opposed to me stopping by for no more than five to 10 minutes, just to ask you a few quick questions and show you what we're doing with other businesses in your area.

You confirm the day and time and move on to the next appointment.

Depending upon the industry you serve and how well your

prospects know one another, you can choose to reference your confirmed appointment or not.

I recommend that you start by referencing your confirmed appointment to see if it helps you land additional appointments. Then try to set the appointment without doing this. Then, you can judge for yourself whether this is to your advantage.

The key takeaway here is the principle of assuming the appointment, instead of cold-call door-knocking.

You'll always want to reach out to those who don't call you back two to three days before the assumptive appointment time to confirm.

Here's a sample script:

CONFIRMING APPOINTMENT

Bob, this is Brian Robinson with The Selling Formula. My number is 555-455-4455. I'm just calling to confirm our appointment for Tuesday, May 5th, at 10:00 a.m. If that time doesn't work, if you would please let me know, I'd appreciate it. Otherwise, I look forward to seeing you then. Thanks, Bob.

If you catch your prospect instead of going to voicemail, you'd say the following:

> Hi Bob, quick question; this is Brian Robinson with The Selling Formula and I'm touching base to confirm our appointment for Tuesday, May 5th, at 10:00 a.m.

Pause and wait for a response from the prospect.

Responses can be interesting here. Sometimes they'll say they never got a voicemail from you and don't know what you're talking about, or they remember the call and that time works for them, or they don't have any interest, or their schedule changed and they won't be available.

Like any good salesperson, you'll need to think quickly and provide a great response, either to capture a potential opportunity or move on to the next one.

WHAT YOU'LL NEED FOR THIS TO WORK

- Have a prospect list with up-to-date contact information: name, address, phone
- Import your prospect list into mapping software, such as Badger Maps
- Develop a great benefit statement for your script which grabs your prospect's interest

- Write out your scripts and practice them
- Choose key prospects in a geographic area on your map, start calling, and set assumptive appointments

THE MOST IMPORTANT POINTS TO KEEP IN MIND

The scripts I've provided are proven to work. The two most important variables will be your reference to other businesses you serve and the associated benefit statement.

For example, if your niche is community banks, you might say,

We work with hundreds of other community banks around the country and provide a five-step formula that can double your cross-sales within 90 days.

The key is that you need to reference the same vertical market or prospect niche with a specific benefit that will at least pique their curiosity by making them wonder what they may be missing by not meeting with you.

If your niche is dentists, you could say,

We work with hundreds of other dentists around the country and have a proven method that doubles your high margin add-on services in 30 days or less.

Be targeted and specific. Your prospects want a perfect match between their need and your offer.

KEY TAKEAWAYS

What I discovered with this approach is that the most important appointment is the first one you set, which becomes the anchor for all the others. Once that's set, you can start rolling through your prospect map and making phone calls.

Bottom line: out of every 10 calls, I'd book three to five confirmed appointments with prospects who were ready to meet with me.

Obviously, things will vary by industry and offering, but it always beat the cold-call, door-knocking approach.

CHAPTER SUMMARY
PREPARATION:

- Compile your prospect list with addresses, phone numbers, and any other important information.
- Import prospect list into map software.
- Create your unique selling proposition/benefit statement.
- Write out your script and customize it with two key items:

- ◦ Your unique selling proposition/benefit statement; and
- ◦ Your specific niche/vertical-market reference.
- Practice your scripts: record them, listen to them, make them conversational, and own them.
- Target the geographic area you're going to work with and at least five prospects you'll call.

IMPLEMENTATION:

- Choose your target prospects in a specific area that you plan to go to about eight to 10 days in advance.
- Call your target prospects and leave a voicemail for them indicating you'll be in their area on a specific day and time, and that, with their permission, you'll stop by for no more than five to 10 minutes to introduce them to your offering.
- Schedule your anchor appointment.
- Call additional prospects referencing your anchor appointment, if appropriate for your industry/offer.
- If you don't hear anything back from a prospect, leave a follow-up voicemail two to three days ahead of your assumed appointment, confirming the day and time of your meeting.
- Show up at the appointed time.

SAMPLE SCRIPTS:

VOICEMAIL SCRIPT #1

[Prospect's First Name], quick question for you. This is [your name] with [your company]. My number is [XXX-XXX-XXXX] and I'm going to be in [prospect city] next [day, month, date] around [time] in the morning/afternoon and wondered if you would be opposed to me stopping by for no more than five to 10 minutes.

We work with other [prospect's business type] providing [unique benefit statement]. So with your permission, I was going to go ahead and pencil in next [day] to stop by.

Of course, I don't know your schedule, so if that doesn't work, if you could kindly let me know, I would appreciate it. Otherwise, I look forward to seeing you next [day, date, time]. Thanks, [prospect's first name]. Again, my number is [XXX-XXX-XXXX].

LIVE SCRIPT #1

[Prospect's First Name], quick question. This is [your name]. I'm going to be in [prospect city] next [day, month, date] around [time] and wondered if you would be opposed to me stopping by for no more than five to 10 minutes to introduce you to what we're doing with [how many of prospect's business type] in the area.

Pause and wait for response from prospect.

We provide a [unique benefit statement] and I was just wondering if you'd be opposed to me stopping by for no more than five to 10 minutes, just to ask you a few quick questions and show you what we're doing with other [prospect's business type] in your area.

VOICEMAIL SCRIPT REFERENCING ANCHOR APPOINTMENT

[Prospect's First Name], quick question for you. This is [your name] with [your company]. My number is [XXX-XXX-XXXX] and I'm going to be in [prospect city] next [day, month, day] meeting with [name of anchor prospect] at [anchor prospect's business name], and while I'm in the area, I'm wondering if you'd be opposed to me stopping by around [time] for no more than five to 10 minutes.

We work with other [prospect's business type] providing [unique benefit statement]. So, with your permission I was going to go ahead and pencil in next [day] to stop by.

Of course, I don't know your schedule, so if that doesn't work, if you could kindly let me know, I would appreciate it. Otherwise, I look forward to seeing you next [day, date, time]. Thanks, [prospect's first name]. Again, my number is [XXX-XXX-XXXX].

LIVE SCRIPT REFERENCING ANCHOR APPOINTMENT

[Prospect's First Name], quick question. This is [your name] and I'm going to be in [prospect city] next [day, day of the month] meeting with [name of anchor prospect] at [anchor prospect's business name]; and while I'm in the area, I'm wondering if you'd be opposed to me stopping by around [time] for no more than five to 10 minutes to introduce you to what we're doing.

Pause and wait for response from prospect.

We provide a [unique benefit statement] and I was just wondering if you'd be opposed to me stopping by for no more than five to 10 minutes, just to ask you a few quick questions and show you what we're doing with other [prospect's business type] in your area.

APPOINTMENT CONFIRMATION SCRIPT

Voicemail version:

[Prospect's First Name], this is [your name] with [your company name]. My number is [XXX-XXX-XXXX]. I'm just calling to confirm our appointment for [day, month, date, time]. If that time doesn't work, if you would please let me know, I'd appreciate it. Otherwise, I look forward to seeing you then. Thanks, [prospect's first name].

Live version:

[Prospect's First Name], quick question. This is [your name] with [your company name] and I'm touching base to confirm our appointment for [day, month, date, time].

Pause and wait for response from prospect.

ABOUT THE AUTHOR

BRIAN W. ROBINSON has worked in sales and marketing with some of the best-known companies in the world, including Coca-Cola USA and Johnson & Johnson. Upon leaving his corporate career, he helped launch a successful startup where he was the first person in the history of the industry to sell more than $1 million of business in 12 months—entirely by phone. His over two-decades-worth of in-the-trenches, battle-tested, face-to-face and phone-presentation knowledge can benefit virtually anyone, from Fortune 500 companies to entrepreneurial ventures.

31937999R00136

Made in the USA
San Bernardino, CA
09 April 2019